the
ADAPTABLE
APPLE

by

Katherine McIlquham

HEARTS 'N TUMMIES
COOKBOOK CO.

1-800-571-BOOK

© 1997 Katherine McIlquham

This book isn't for the purpose of convincing folks that apples make for super good eating. Anyone who doesn't already know that those round hunks of magic are the finest eating on this side of the Pearly Gates, has been hangin' out on some other planet.

The purpose of this cookbook is to provide the chief cook with some really really great ways to turn those "hunks of magic" into things to eat that'll knock their socks off.

Both Katherine and the editorial staff at Hearts 'N Tummies thank the LaFayette Area Apple Growers Assn. for their valuable input for this book.

Questions frequently asked

WHY ARE SOME APPLES HIGHER PRICED THAN OTHERS?

It's simply supply and demand.

WHAT IS THE DIFFERENCE BETWEEN CIDER AND JUICE?

At present the terms are used interchangeably. In the early 1900s cider was a fermented beverage, but now it's referring to the juice of apples.

HOW DO I KNOW WHEN A PARTICULAR BRAND OF APPLE IS RIPE?

The best way is to refer to our apple chart or call the orchard where you buy your apples. Most orchards will not save apples for you. However, they might notify you when that apple is ready.

WHICH APPLE IS THE BEST TO EAT?

This depends on your taste and desired texture preference. The best way to tell is to ask for a sample to taste. PLEASE do not squeeze or pinch apples to test for firmness, they bruise so easily!

HOW MANY POUNDS OF APPLES IN A PECK?

This depends totally on the kind of apple. The <u>average</u> is 10 lbs., but you are talking volume in pecks, not weight.

IF I LIKE A PIE THAT KEEPS THE SLICE, WHAT KIND OF APPLE SHOULD I BUY?

Refer to the chart in this book or ask your sales clerk at the orchard. Generally, apples early in the season mush more than those picked near the end of the season.

WHEN YOU PLANT AN APPLE TREE HOW LONG BEFORE IT BEARS FRUIT?

This depends on the rootstock and age of the tree purchased. Trees will produce fruit within a few years, but on the average for a tree to be full bearing, it might be 10 years. Properly cared for apple trees will bear fruit for as long as 100 years; there are some trees in our area that are that old.

WHY DIDN'T MY APPLE TREE HAVE APPLES THIS YEAR. WE HAD LOTS LAST YEAR?

The orchards control the amount of blossoms on a tree by spray so that the trees don't overbear one year and have to rest the next.

WHEN SHOULD I PRUNE MY APPLE TREES?

Most pruning is usually done in the winter while the tree is dormant. Tips on pruning can be obtained from your local extension office.

Cooking and Storage Tips:

For a sugarless pie, thaw 1 (6 oz.) can frozen unsweetened apple juice concentrate or use 3/4 c. fresh apple cider. Combine with 2 T. flour and 1 tsp. cinnamon in a container with a tight lid. Shake well. Pour into a saucepan; cook over medium heat until the mixture boils and thickens. Remove from heat. Add 6 c. sliced, peeled apples to the hot mixture; stir to coat. Spoon into pie shell and bake as usual.

For a tasty variation to your favorite apple crisp recipe, try adding a handful of raisins.

When making an apple pie, add the required amount of sugar to the apple slices immediately after first slicing. This prevents the fruit from browning before baking.

For moist and colorful poultry stuffing, add 1 diced, unpeeled apple to your favorite stuffing mixture.

As a topping for pancakes or waffles, heat together 1 c. applesauce and 1 c. maple syrup.

For sugarless applesauce, omit the sugar and just add cinnamon for flavor.

When you make stuffing on the stove instead of in the turkey, put an apple in the turkey cavity to keep it moist.

To prevent crust from burning when baking an apple pie, microwave the apple, cinnamon sugar mixture first for 10 minutes, stir, then 10 more minutes. Then place the filling into the pie crust and continue as usual, baking the pie until the crust is done.

To soften brown sugar, add an apple slice and reseal.

After school snack sandwiches are great when made of rye bread, sliced cheese and apple slices or white bread, peanut butter and apple slices.

Ideal storage conditions for apples are around 35F with a humidity of 85%. The best place for long term storage is in the refrigerator.

If you don't have enough refrigerator storage, get apples on a cool brisk day and store in your garage in a picnic or plastic cooler.

For long-term storage, wrap unbruised, individual apples in tissue paper or newspaper. This does not keep them longer; however, if one does spoil it will not affect the one stored next to it.

To keep cookies moist, place an apple in the bottom of the cookie jar.

To prevent discoloration of apples, place peeling apple slices in a pan of cold water to which a pinch of salt has been added for each apple peeled, or slice into water with 1 T. of lemon juice.

Sprinkle the apple slices with lemon juice for white apples in salads.

The Cortland is known as the salad apple because it stays white when peeled.

If your aluminum pans need brightening, boil some apple peelings in them and they will again become shiny on the inside.

If your apple pie runs over in the oven, sprinkle the drippings with salt while still warm and this will make it easier to clean the oven.

When making applesauce it is often better to mix several kinds of apples for better flavor.

Too much sugar added to apple dishes spoils the natural flavor of the food and also tends to make the apples mushy.

CALORIE COUNTER

Apple butter, 1 T.   =   33
Apple cider, 1 c.   = 117
Apples: Fresh, w/skin, avg. 2-1/2" diam. = 61
               dried, cooked, sweetened, 1/2 c. = 157
               dried, cooked, unsweetened, 1/2 c. = 100
Applesauce, canned sweetened, 1/2 c. = 116
Applesauce, canned unsweetened, 1/2 c. = 50
Apple pie - baked, 3-1/8" arc (1/8 or an 8" pie) = 173

NUTRIENTS in one medium-sized apple
(2" diameter - 150 grams or 1/3 lb.)

Source: USDA Handbook #8

BASIC FOOD COMPONENTS
(Approx.)
Protein -- .3 grams
Fat -- .9 grams
Carbohydrates -- 21.0 grams

MINERALS
(Approx.)
Calcium -- 10.5 milligrams
Phosphorus -- 15.0 milligrams
Iron -- .45 milligrams
Potassium -- 165.0 milligrams
Sodium -- 1.5 milligrams
Magnesium -- 12.0 milligrams

OTHER COMPONENTS

Fiber -- 1.5 grams
Pectin -- 1.2 grams
Food Energy -- 87 calories
Ash -- .45 grams
Water -- 85%

VITAMINS
(Approx.)
A -- 135.0 (Int'l Units)
B -- (Thiamine) .04 milligrams
Niacin -- .15 milligrams
C (ascorbic acid) -- 6.0 milligrams
Riboflavin -- .03 milligrams

Apple Arithmetic:
1 bushel apples   = 16 quart of applesauce.
1 peck apples   = 4 to 5 pies.
1 lb. apples   = 3 medium apples
10 lb. apples   = 1 peck
40 lb. apples   = 1 bushel
1 medium apple   = 1 c. chopped apple
1 lb. apples   = 3 c. diced apples
1 lb. apples   = 1-1/2 c. applesauce
2 lb. apples   = 1 - 9" apple pie

VARIETY	FLAVOR/TEXTURE	EATING FRESH	BAKING/DESSERTS	PIE	SAUCE	FREEZING/CANNING	
DUCHESS	TART				X	X	EX FOR SAUCE
WHITNEY CRAB	SWEET	X	X		X		GOOD PICKLED
BEACON	MED-SWEET	X	X	X	X	X	GREAT BAKING
PAULA RED	TART/JUICY	X	X	X	X	X	MUSHES WELL
WEALTHY	NIPPY/FIRM	X	X	X	X	X	ALL PURPOSE
EMPIRE	SWEET/JUICY	X	X	X	X	X	EX EATING
RED BARON	SWEET/JUICY	X	X	X	X	X	EX SAUCE
MC INTOSH	SPICYSWEET/JUICY	X	X	X	X	X	MOST TENDER APPLE
HONEYGOLD	SWEET/FIRM	X	X	X	X		SIMILAR TO DELICIOUS
CHESTNUT CRAB	SWEET/JUICY	X				X	GREAT SNACKS
CORTLAND	SLIGHTLYTART/ MED	X	X	X	X	X	STAYS WHITE
REDWELL	SWEET/DRY	X	X	X	X	X	EX PIE
FIRESIDE	SWEET/FIRM	X	X	X	X	X	GOOD KEEPERS
CONNELL RED	SWEET/SOLID	X	X	X		X	KEEPS SHAPE
HARALSON	TART/JUICY	X	X	X	X	X	GREAT CARAMELING
PRARIE SPY	MOD.TART/FIRM	X	X	X	X	X	FIRM IN PIE
NORTHWEST. GREENING	TART/FIRM	X	X	X		X	SWEETEN W/ AGE
SPARTAN	MILDY TART/CRISP	X	X	X	X	X	GOOD EATING
REGENT	SWEET/JUICY	X	X	X	X	X	EX FOR KEEPING
WOLF RIVER	MILD/DRY		X	X	X	X	GREAT FOR PIE
KEEPSAKE	TART/FIRM	X		X		X	GOOD KEEPER
SWEET 16	SWEET/JUICY	X	X	X	X	X	NEEDS LITTLE SUGAR

CIDER

People have been making and consuming apple cider since the first apple tree planted by Governor Endicott of the Massachusett's Bay Colony in 1629 began to bear fruit. Since every apple is more than 80% juice, apple cider is also a part of our culinary heritage. As the juice stood for any length of time under usual conditions, it fermented, increasing its appeal to many people. Hard cider became a popular substitute when the early wars cut off America's supply of imported French wines. It wasn't until the 1940s that techniques were perfected for packing pasteurized apple juice/cider.

Most roadside markets offer non-pasteurized juice/cider. This is natural, undiluted, unfermented, unsweetened juice from whole clean, fresh, ripe apples of at least three different varieties for proper flavor. Flavor refers to the degree of excellence and palatability typical of apple juice that has been properly processed. Flavor, therefore will vary in different geographical areas. The color is usually cloudy. Cloudy cider contains more pectin and apple solids. Preservatives may or may not be added. This cider needs constant refrigeration and will stay sweet and unfermented for one to two weeks or two to three weeks if preservative has been added. If it is not going to be consumed in this time, it can easily be frozen for future use. It is usually available in 1/2 gallon and gallon containers.

Table of Contents

BARS AND COOKIES

Apple Cream Cheese Bars

Crust:
2 c. flour	3 T. oil
3 T. sugar	1 sm. egg
1 t. salt	2-2/3 T. cold water
1/3 c. butter	

Filling:
6 c. apples, pared and sliced	1/2 c. flour
	2 t. lemon rind, grated
1 c. sugar	1 T. lemon juice

Topping:
40 caramels	1 egg
1 c. evaporated milk	1/3 c. sugar
8-oz. soft cream cheese	1/2 c. chopped nuts

Crust: Combine flour, sugar and salt, cut in butter. Blend in oil, egg and cold water until mixture reaches pie-crust consistency. Roll in rectangle and place in a jelly roll or 9"x13" pan.

Filling: Combine apples, sugar, flour, lemon rind and lemon juice; place on crust. Melt caramels in the evaporated milk. Pour mixture over the apple filling. Combine cheese, egg and sugar. Spread over the caramel topping. Sprinkle nuts over the cream cheese mix. Bake at 325F for 55 min. Makes 20-24 bars.

Johnny Appleseed is a real person.
He was born in 1774 in Leominster, Mass.
He traveled about the new territories leasing land and
developing nurseries of fruit trees.
He died at the age of 71 at Fort Wayne, Indiana.
At the time of death he had accumulated
1,200 acres of orchard.

Apple Pie Bars

Crust:
2 c. flour
1/2 c. sugar (opt)
1/2 t. baking powder
1/2 t. salt
1 c. butter
2 egg yolks, beaten

Filling:
4 c. pared, cored and sliced apples (1/8" thick)
1/2 c. sugar
1/4 c. flour
1 t. cinnamon
1/4 t. nutmeg
2 egg whites, slightly beaten

Combine flour, sugar, baking powder and salt; cut in butter as for pie crust. Mix in egg yolks (mixture will be crumbly) Press 1/2 of the mixture in bottom of 15"x10" jelly roll pan. (May also use 13"x9"x2" pan) Set remaining 1/2 of the mixture aside. Combine all of filling ingredients except egg whites; arrange over bottom crust. Crumble remaining crust mixture over filling. Brush egg whites over all. Bake at 350F for 30 min. (jelly roll pan) or 40 min. (13"x9"x2" pan) Cool. Drizzle with thin confectioners sugar glaze, if desired. Yield: 3-4 dozen bars.

Applesauce Cookies

1 c. raisins	1 t. baking soda
1 c. applesauce	1 t. cinnamon
1 c. brown sugar	1/2 t. nutmeg
1/2 c. butter	1/4 t. cloves
1 egg	1/2 t. salt
2 c. flour	

Beat butter, sugar and egg. Mix baking soda with apple-sauce. Then add to butter mixture. Add flour and spices. Stir in raisins. Bake on greased cookie sheet at 375F for 8-10 min. Cool and ice with butter frosting.

Butter Frosting:

1/3 c. butter	1/4 c. milk
4-1/2 c. powdered sugar	1-1/2 t. vanilla

Beat butter till fluffy. Gradually add 2 c. of the powdered sugar; beat well. Slowly beat in the 1/4 c. milk and vanilla. Beat in remaining sugar. Beat in additional milk if needed, to make of spreading consistency.

Apple Hermits

1/2 c. butter or margarine	1/2 t. soda
1 c. pkd. brown sugar	1/2 t. salt
1 egg	1/2 t. cinnamon
1/4 c. milk	1/4 t. ground cloves
2 c. unsifted all-purpose flour	1/2 c. chopped nuts
	2 c. peeled, shredded apples (about 2)

In a lg. bowl, cream butter and sugar. Beat in egg and milk. Mix flour, soda, salt, cinnamon and cloves. Blend into creamed mixture. Stir in nuts and apples. Drop by T. on greased baking sheet. Bake in 375F oven for 10-14 min. Cool on racks. Makes about 3-1/2 dozen.

Apple Cinnamon Squares

3/4 c. flour
1/3 t. baking soda
1/3 t. cinnamon
1/8 t. salt
1/3 c. butter
2/3 c. sugar

1 lg. egg, beaten
1/3 t. vanilla
1-3/4 c. baking apples,
    pared and chopped
1/2 c. nuts, chopped

Combine flour, baking soda, cinnamon and salt. Beat butter, sugar, egg and vanilla extract with an electric beater for 3 min. Add dry ingredients in a sm. amount and beat after each addition. Stir in apples and nuts. Pour the batter in a greased jelly roll pan. Bake in a 350F oven for 40 min. or until done. Cool. Frost with vanilla glaze.

"Vanilla Glaze":
2 T. butter, softened   2 T. milk
1-1/2 c. powdered sugar

Whip butter until creamy. Add the powdered sugar and milk and beat until smooth. Spread glaze over bars.

A spiral of apple peeling,
thrown over the shoulder of an unmarried peeler,
supposedly will form the initial of her future husband.

Apple Brownie w/Caramel Sauce

1/4 c. butter
1 c. sugar
1 egg
1 c. flour

1 t. baking soda
2 c. chopped apples
1/2 c. nuts
1/2 c. raisins
1 t. cinnamon

Sauce:
1/2 c. brown sugar
1/2 c. white sugar

1/2 c. butter
1/2 c. cream

Cream butter, 1 c. sugar and egg; add flour, soda, apples, nuts, raisins and cinnamon. Put in deep muffin tins. Bake 20-25 min at 350F. Makes 12 lg. muffins. Combine sauce ingredients and boil several min. Serve over brownies warm or cold.

APPLE A DAY

Long before the medical profession knew anything about preventive medicine, proverbial wisdon taught that an apple a day kept the doctor away. This rhyming proverb is more generative than curative.

1. An apple one day kept Paradise away.
2. An apple a day keeps the doctor away,
   but not if it's green.
3. During retirement a nap a day keeps the doctor away.
4. An apple a day keeps the doctor away,
   but an onion a day keeps everyone away.
5. An apple a day keeps the ear, eye, nose, and throat specialist, the dermatologist, and the gastroenterologist away.

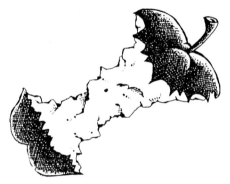

Apple (Fresh) Cookies

1/2 c. butter
1-1/3 c. brown sugar
1 egg
2 c. flour
1 t. baking soda
1/2 t. salt
2 c. finely chopped unpeeled apples

1/2 t. cinnamon
1 t. ground cloves
1/2 t. nutmeg
1 c. chopped nuts
1 c. raisins
1/4 c. apple cider

Cream butter, sugar and egg. Sift dry ingredients together and add to creamed mixture. Mix alternately with cider, apples and nuts. Drop onto greased cookie sheet and bake 8-10 min. at 375F.

Apple Date Squares

1/2 c. shortening
2/3 c. sugar
1 egg
1-1/2 c. flour

1 t. baking soda
1/4 t. salt
2 c. diced apples
1 c. snipped dates

Topping:
1/2 c. brown sugar
1 t. cinnamon

1/2 c. chopped nuts

In a lg. bowl, cream shortening and sugar till light and fluffy. Add egg and beat well. Mix flour, soda and salt together; beat into creamed mixture. Fold in apples and dates. Pour into greased and floured 10"x6"x2" baking dish. Lightly pat topping on top of batter. Bake at 350F for 30-40 min. Cut in squares and serve with ice cream or whipped cream.

Apple Brownies

2/3 c. butter	2 c. flour
2 c. brown sugar	2 t. baking powder
2 eggs	1/4 t. salt
1 t. vanilla	1 c. chopped apples
1/2 c. nuts	confectioners' sugar

Cream butter and brown sugar. Add eggs, vanilla, mixing well. Combine flour, baking powder and salt. Add slowly to creamed mixture. Add chopped apples and nuts. Pour into well-greased 12"x9" pan. Bake at 350 degrees for 35 minutes. When cool, sprinkle with confectioners' sugar.

Apple pie without cheese,
is like a hug,
without a squeeze.

Apples are thought to quench the flame of Venus,
according to that old English saying,
He that will not a wife wed,
Must eat a cold apple when he goeth to bed,
though some turn it to a contrary purpose.

Ait a happle avore gwain to bed,
An' you'll make the doctor beg his bread.
or, as the more popular version runs: An apple a
day keeps the doctor away.

Eat an apple on going to bed,
And you'll keep the doctor from earning his bread.

Apple Bars

Mix together:	1 c. flour
	1/2 t. salt
	1/2 t. baking soda
Cut in:	1/2 c. shortening
Add:	1/2 c. brown sugar
	1 c. quick oatmeal

Put 1/2 the mixture in the bottom of a 8" sq. pan.
Add: 3-1/2 c. of apples
                        3/4 c. sugar

Dot with butter and cinnamon. Cover with the rest of the crumbs. Bake at 350F for 30-40 min.

Apple Squares, Snowy Glazed

2-1/2 c. sifted flour
1/2 t. salt
1 c. shortening
2 eggs, separated
milk

1-1/2 c. crushed cornflakes
5 c. sliced Haralson apples
1 c. sugar
1-1/2 t. cinnamon

Glaze:
1-1/4 c. powdered sugar
3 T. water

1/2 t. vanilla

Combine flour and salt in bowl. Cut in shortening. In a measuring cup, beat egg yokes with enough milk to make 2/3 c. Toss lightly with flour. Divide almost in half. Roll larger portion to fit 15"x9" jelly roll pan. Sprinkle with cornflakes, spread over apples. Combine sugar and cinnamon. Sprinkle over apples. Roll out remining dough and place on top, seal edges. Beat whites until foamy, spread on crust. Bake at 350F for 1 hr. Cool slightly; spread with glaze.

Glaze: Combine 1-1/4 c. confectioner's sugar, water and vanilla.

Apple Granola

1/2 c. butter	1 c. dried apples, cubed
1/2 c. brown sugar	1/2 c. grated coconut
4 c. minute oatmeal, uncooked	3/4 c. broken walnut pieces
1/2 c. dates, chopped	dash of salt

Melt butter in lg. skillet over med. heat. (If using electric skillet, set at 325F.) Add brown sugar, stir until dissolved. Combine remaining ingredients and stir into butter mixture. Continue to cook for about 10 min., stirring occasionally. Transfer granola to lg. bowl. Store in a tightly covered container.

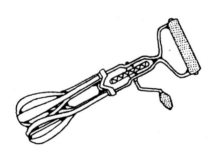

Apple Squares

2 c. flour	6 c. apples, sliced
1/2 t. salt	1 c. sugar
3/4 c. shortening	1 T. cornstarch
1 egg or 2 egg whites	1 c. water
3 T. water	1 t. cinnamon

Mix flour, salt, cut shortening into particles the size of sm. peas. Combine egg, water, toss lightly until evenly moistened. Roll out 1/2 of dough, put in bottom of 13"x9"x2" pan. Fill with apples. Combine sugar, cornstarch, water, pour over apples, sprinkle with cinnamon. Roll out remianing dough put on top of apples. Bake at 400F for 15 min. Then at 350F for 30 min. or until done. When cooled, frost with icing if desired.

Icing:
1/2 c. confectioner's sugar	1/4 t. vanilla
2 t. butter	4-5 t. milk

Apple Coconut Cookies

1 c. flour
1/2 t. baking powder
1/2 t. baking soda
1/2 t. salt
1/2 c. butter or margarine,
　　room temperature
1/2 c. granulated sugar

1/2 c. pkd. brown sugar
1 t. vanilla
1 egg
1/2 c. oats
1 c. chopped peeled apple
2 c. flaked coconut

Mix flour, baking soda, baking powder, and salt. Beat butter; gradually beat in sugars until light and fluffy. Blend in egg and vanilla. Blend in flour mixture. Add oats, apple and 1-1/3 c. coconut. Drop from t. onto ungreased baking sheet. Sprinkle with remaining coconut. Bake at 375F for about 10", or until golden brown.

Applesauce Cookies

1/2 c. margarine or butter, softened
3/4 c. applesauce
2-3/4 c. flour
1-1/2 c. pkd brown sugar

1 c. chopped pecans
1 t. salt
1 t. vanilla
1/2 t. baking soda
2 eggs

If using self-rising flour, omit salt and baking soda.
Heat oven to 375F. Mix margarine and applesauce. Stir in remaining ingredients. Drop dough by rounded t. about 1" apart onto ungreased cookie sheet. Bake until almost no indentation remains when touched, 8-10 min. Immediately remove from cookie sheet; cool. Frost with caramel frosting.

Caramel Frosting:
1/2 c. margarine or butter
1 c. pkd brown sugar

1/4 c. milk
2 . powdered sugar

Heat margarine in 2 qt. saucepan until melted. Stir in brown sugar. Heat to boiling, stirring constantly. Boil and stir over low heat 2 min., stir in milk. Heat to boiling; remove from heat. Cool to lukewarm. Gradually stir in powdered sugar. Place pan of frosting in bowl of cold water; beat until smooth and of spreading consistency. If frosting becomes too stiff, stir in additional milk, 1 t. at a time.

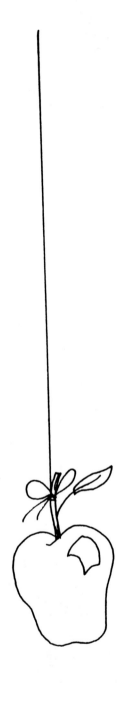

Apple Lemon Bread

2 c. flour	2/3 c. sugar
1 t. baking soda	2 eggs, slightly beaten
1 t. baking powder	2 c. shredded, peeled apple
3/4 t. salt	4 t. grated lemon peel
1/4 c. butter	2/3 c. chopped nuts

Mix flour, baking soda, baking powder and salt; set aside. Cream butter and sugar until light and fluffy; beat in eggs until blended. Add flour mixture alternately with apple, blending well. Stir in lemon peel and nuts. Turn into greased and floured 9"x5" loaf pan. Bake at 350F for 50-60 min., or until toothpick inserted in center comes out clean. Cool in pan on rack.

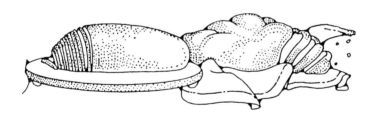

Apple Muffins

1 c. shortening	1 c. sugar
3 c. flour	1 c. milk
2 eggs	1 t. cinnamon
2 T. baking powder	1 t. salt
1 c. apple chunks	

Cream together shortening and sugar. Add other ingredients except apples. Cut apple in sm. chunks and add to mixture. Place in muffin pan and bake at 375F for 20 min.

Apple (Fresh) Fruitcake

1 8-oz. pkg. chopped dates	1 c. chopped nuts
3 c. flour	1 t. baking soda
3 eggs	1 t. cinnamon
1-1/2 c. oil	2 t. vanilla
2 c. sugar	1 can flakes coconut
3 c. chopped apples	1 c. chopped maraschino cherries

Beat eggs until thick; gradually add sugar, oil, flour with cinnamon, soda and vanilla. Stir in dates, coconut, cherries, nuts and chopped apples. Bake in a greased and floured 10" tube tin at 300F for about 1-1/2 hrs. Great gift for the holidays.

Apple Muffins, Hearty

1-1/4 c. skim milk
2 egg whites
1/4 c. honey OR
   brown sugar
2 T. vegetable oil

1 apple, peeled, cored and
   diced
2-1/2 c. oat bran
1 T. baking powder
1/4 c. raisins

Preheat oven to 400F. In a blender, combine milk, egg whites, honey OR brown sugar, oil and apple, blending well. In a med. bowl, add remaining ingredients and mix well. Add blended mixture to dry mixture. Fill muffin pan sprayed with cooking spray, 2/3 full with batter. Bake 12-14 min.

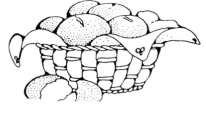

Apple Streusel Muffins

2 c. flour
1 c. sugar
1 T. baking powder
1-1/4 t. cinnamon
1/2 t. salt
1/2 t. baking soda

2 lg. eggs, beaten
1 c. sour cream
1/4 c. butter, melted
1 c. finely diced apples,
   unpeeled

Streusel Topping:
1/4 c. sugar
3 T. flour

1/4 t. cinnamon
2 T. butter

In a lg. bowl, stir together flour, sugar, baking powder, cinnamon, salt and baking soda; set aside. In a sm. bowl, beat eggs, sour cream and butter. Add all at once to dry ingredients along with apples. Stir just until moistened. Fill well-greased muffin tins 2/3 full. (I have also used paper cup cake liners, do not grease tins.)

Combine topping ingredients; sprinkle on. Bake at 400F for 20-25 min. Yield: 18 muffins.

Apple (Spiced) Loaf

3 c. flour
1 t. baking powder
1 t. baking soda
1/2 t. salt
1 t. cinnamon
1/2 t. nutmeg
1-1/2 c. sugar

3 eggs
1/2 c. vegetable oil
1/2 c. sour milk
2 c. apples, peeled and
    grated
1/2 c. chopped nuts
1 t. vanilla

In a lg. mixing bowl, sift the dry ingredients and mix together. Make a well in the center and add eggs, oil and sour milk; mix well. Blend in apples, nuts and vanilla. Pour batter into 2 greased 9"x5"x3" loaf pans and bake at 325F for 55-60 min. Remove from pans and cool on rack. Servings: 2 loaves. Preparation time: 1-1/4 hr.

Applesauce Nut Bread

2 c. flour
3/4 c. sugar
1 t. baking powder
1 t. salt
1/2 t. baking soda

1/2 t. nutmeg
1 c. chopped nuts
1 egg
1 c. applesauce

Combine ingredients enough to moisten and bake in greased loaf pan. Bake 1 hr. at 350F.

Apple Bread

1 c. sugar
1/2 c. shortening
2 eggs OR 4 egg whites
1-1/2 t. milk (sweet or sour)
    put 1 t. soda in milk

2 c. flour
1 t. vanilla
1 c. grated apples

Mix accordingly, use all juice from apples. Add nuts if desired. Bake at 350F for 1 hr.

Apple Raisin Pancakes

2 c. flour
2 T. sugar
2-1/2 t. baking powder
2 t. cinnamon
1-3/4 c. skim milk

1/2 c. egg substitute
1/4 c. melted margarine
3/4 c. pared, chooped apple
3/4 c. raisisns

Combine dry ingredients. Beat together milk, egg substitute
and melted margarine; stir into dry ingredients. Stir in apple
and raisins. Cook on a lightly greased griddle over med.-
high heat, using 1/4 c. batter for each pancake. Makes
about 15 4" pancakes.

Apple Zucchini Bread

4 c. all-purpose flour
1 T. baking soda
1/4 t. baking powder
1-1/2 t. salt
1-1/2 T. ground cinnamon
1/2 t. ground nutmeg
5 eggs
2 c. sugar

1 c. pkd. brown sugar
1-1/2 c. vegetable oil
1 T. vanilla extract
2 c. shredded zucchini,
   about 3 med.
1 c. shredded apple,
   about 1 med.
1-1/2 c. chopped pecans

Combine first 6 ingredients; set aside. Combine eggs, sugars, oil and vanilla in a lg. bowl; beat at med. speed of an electric mixer until well-blended. Stir in zucchini, apple, and pecans. Add dry ingredients to zucchini-apple mixture, stirring just until moistened.

Spoon batter into 3 greased and floured 8-1/4"x4-1/2"x3" loaf pans. Bake at 350F for 50-55 min. or until a wooden pick inserted in center comes out clean. Cool in pans 10 min; remove to wire rack, and cool completely. Yield: 3 loaves.

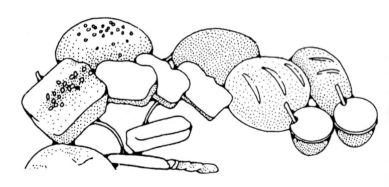

Apple (Fresh) Bread

2 c. flour
1 t. baking soda
1 t. baking powder
1/2 t. salt
1 t. cinnamon
1/2 c. shortening

1 c. sugar
2 eggs
1-1/2 c. baking apples, chopped
1/2 c. nuts, chopped
1 t. vanilla

Stir first 5 ingredients together. Cream shortening, sugar and eggs. Add apples, nuts and vanilla. Stir in flour mixture. Pour batter into 9"x5"x3" bread pan. Sprinkle with a topping mixture of 1/4 c. sugar and 1-1/2 t. cinnamon. Bake at 350F for 1 hr. Yield: 1 loaf.

Apple Muffins

1 egg
1 c. milk
1/4 c. melted shortening
2/3 c. sugar
1/2 t. salt
1/4 t. cinnamon

1 t. lemon juice
1/4 t. vanilla
2 c. sifted flour
3 t. baking powder
1 c. chopped apples

Beat eggs; stir in milk, shortening, sugar, salt, cinnamon, lemon juice and vanilla. Sift together flour and baking powder. Stir into milk mixture just until blended. Do not over mix. Fold in apples. Fill greased muffin cups 2/3 full. Bake at 450F about 20 min. or until brown.

A person who gains favor by flattery
is known as an apple polisher.

Applesauce Loaf

1/2 c. butter, softened	3/4 t. nutmeg
1 c. sugar	1/2 t. salt
1 egg	1/2 t. ground cloves
1-1/2 c. flour	1-1/4 c. applesauce
1-1/2 t. baking soda	1/2 c. raisins
1 t. cinnamon	1/2 c. chopped walnuts

Cream butter and sugar until light. Beat in egg. Stir together flour, baking soda, cinnamon, nutmeg, salt and cloves. Gradually add to creamed mixture. Beat applesauce into batter. Stir in raisins and nuts. Pour into greased and floured 9"x5" loaf pan. Bake at 350F for 1 hr. Cool in pan 10 min. Remove from pan, cool on wire rack. Sprinkle with powdered sugar. Makes 1 loaf.

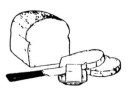

Apple Oatmeal

Kids Favorite !

4 c. water	1 c. apple, chopped and
1 t. salt (Opt.)	peeled
2 T. butter	1/2 c. raisins
2 c. old fash. rolled oats	1/4 t. nutmeg
	1/2 t. cinnamon

Combine 4 c. water, 1 t. salt and 2 T. butter in lg. saucepan; bring to full boil. Stir in 2 c. old fashioned rolled oats, 1 c. of chopped, peeled apple, 1/2 c. raisins, 1/2 t. cinnamon and 1/4 t. nutmeg. Cook 5 min. at med. heat, stirring occasionally. Cover; remove from heat. Let stand 2-3 min. before serving.

Fruity Muffins

1 c. all-purpose flour	3/4 c. brown sugar
1/2 c. quick oats	1/4 c. margarine, melted
1 t. baking powder	1 t. vanilla
1 t. ground cinnamon	3/4 c. diced apple
1/4 t. slat	3/4 c. fresh cranberries
1 egg	1/4 c. raisins

Heat oven to 350F. Grease muffin tins. Mix flour, oats, baking powder, cinnamon and salt in a lg. bowl. Break egg into another bowl. Add sugar and mix with egg until smooth. Add in melted margarine and vanilla. Stir in apple, cranberries and raisins. Pour over dry ingredients. Fold in just until dry ingredients are moistened. Spoon batter into muffin cups. Bake 20-25 min. Do not freeze these muffins.

Lemon Apple Oat Muffins

1 egg
1/2 c. milk
1/4 c. vegetable oil
2 T. bottled lemon juice
3/4 c. quick cooking oats
1-1/4 c. unsifted flour
1/2 c. firmly packed
   brown sugar

1-1/2 t. baking powder
1 t. baking soda
1 t. ground cinnamon
1/2 t. salt
1/4 t. ground nutmeg
1 c. finely chopped baking
   apple (about 1 med.)

Lemon Icing:
1/2 c. powdered sugar
1 T. lemon juice

1 T. melted butter OR
   margarine

Preheat oven to 400F. In a med. bowl, beat egg. Stir in milk, oil and then lemon juice. Add oats; mix well. Combine flour, brown sugar, baking powder, baking soda, cinnamon, salt and nutmeg. Add to oats mixture with apples and nuts. Mix only until moistened. (Batter will be very thick.) Spoon into muffin cups that are greased or lined with paper baking cups. Bake for 20 min., or until golden. ·

Make frosting by combining powdered sugar, lemon juice and butter. Spoon over hot muffins. Remove from tins. Makes about 1 dozen.

To tell the course of true love · slice an apple in two.
Count the seeds in each half.
If each has an equal number of seeds,
a marriage will follow soon;
if one of the seeds was cut in two,
the course of love will not be smooth.

CAKES

Apple Walnut Cake, Spiced

3/4 c. raisins
2 T. rum or brandy
1 c. butter, room temp.
1 c. sugar
3 lg. eggs
3 c. flour
1-1/2 t. baking soda

1/2 t. each: nutmeg, cinnamon, salt
1/4 t. each: ginger, allspice, mace
3-1/2 c. coarsely chopped apples (about 1 lb.)
1 c. chopped walnuts
12 whole walnuts

Mix raisins and rum; set aside. In a lg. mixing bowl, beat butter and sugar until light and creamy. Add eggs, 1 at a time, beating until blended. Stir together flour, soda, nutmeg, cinnamon, salt, ginger, allspice and mace. Add to butter mixture 1/2 at a time, mixing to blend. Stir in raisins and rum, apples and chopped walnuts just until well distributed. Spread batter into a buttered and floured 2" deep, 10" diamter cake pan with removable rim; arrange whole walnuts over top. Bake in a 325F oven until toothpick inserted in center comes out clean, about an hr. Cool in pan on a rack. Remove rim. Serve hot of cold. Cut into wedges. Serves 12 455 calorie per serving.

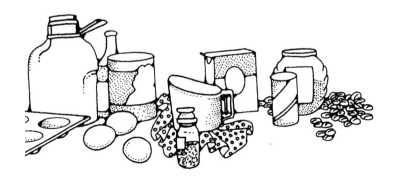

Applesauce Bran Snack Cake

2 c. flour
1/2 c. 100% bran
4 t. baking powder
1-1/2 t. cinnamon
1/2 t. nutmeg
1/2 t. allspice

1/4 c. egg substitute
  (ex: egg beaters)
1 c. applesauce
3/4 c. brown sugar
1/2 c. softened margarine
2/3 c. raisins
powdered sugar

Combine dry ingredients. Add egg substitute, applesauce, brown sugar, and margarine. Beat at med. speed for 2 min. Stir in raisins. Spread in a greased and floured 8"x8" baking pan. Bake at 350F for 35-40 min., or until done. Dust with powdered sugar when cool. Makes 9 servings.

There's plenty of boys that will come hankering and
gruvvelling around when you've got an apple,
and beg the core off you;
but when they've got one,
and you beg for the core,
and remind then how you give them a core one time,
they make a mouth at you,
and say thank you 'most to death,
but there ain't a-going to be no core.

Apple Sour Cream Bundt Cake

1/2 c. chopped walnuts
1 t. cinnamon
1/2 c. sugar
1/2 c. butter
1 c. sugar
2 c. flour

1-1/2 c. finely chopped
  apples, peeled
1 c. sour cream
2 eggs
1 t. baking powder
1 t. baking soda
1 t. vanilla

Cinnamon Carmel Glaze/Sauce:
3/4 c. brown sugar
2 T. butter

1/2 t. cinnamon
1/3 c. hot evaporated milk

Combine nuts, cinnamon and sugar, in sm. bowl; set aside. In lg. bowl cream butter and sugar until light and fluffy. Add flour, sour cream, eggs, baking powder, soda and vanilla; beat 3 min. Prepare the apples; set aside. Grease and lightly flour a bundt pan. Spread 1/2 of the batter in a pan; sprinkle with 1/2 of nut mixture, then chopped apples. Sprinkle remaining nut mixture over apples then spread remaining batter over top. Bake at 350F for 60 min. or until cake begins to pull away from sides of pan. Make glaze by putting all of the ingredients in a blender, covering and processing on high until sugar is dissolved; set aside. Cool cake slightly on rack; remove from pan. Drizzle glaze/sauce over cake. Yield: 12-16 servings.

Apple Pecan Cake, Chunky

3 c. flour
2 t. cinnamon
1 t. baking soda
1 t. salt
1 c. vegetable oil
1/2 c. unsalted butter,
    melted

2 c. pkd brown sugar
3 lg. eggs
2 t. vanilla
3 c. cubed tart apples
1-1/2 c. pecan halves
1 c. golden raisins

Heat oven to 350F. Butter and flour 10" tube or bundt pan. Sift flour, cinnamon, baking soda and salt together. Beat oil, butter, sugar, eggs and vanilla in lg. mixer bowl until creamy. Stir in dry ingredients. (Batter will be very thick.) Fold in apples, pecans and raisins, spoon onto prepared pan and smooth top. Bake until wooden pick inserted in center comes out clean, about 1-1/2 hr. Let cool completely in pan. Invert onto platter and cut into wedges.

Applesauce Cake, Chocolate

1 pkg. Devil's food cake mix, 2 layer size

2 eggs
2 c. applesauce
peanut butter

Mix and bake cake according to pkg. directions, using applesauce in place of water. Spread a thin layer of peanut butter on the cake while it's still slightly warm. Frost cooled.

Apple-Raisin-Walnut Cake

3 eggs
1 c. vegetable oil
2 c. sugar
1 t. vanilla
4 c. grated apples,
    unpeeled
2 c. sifted flour

1 t. baking soda
1/2 t. salt
1 t. cloves
1 t. cinnamon
1/2 c. raisins
3/4 c. chopped walnuts

Beat eggs and oil together in a mixing bowl until foamy; add sugar and vanilla and continue to beat. Add apples, beat slightly; set aside. Sift together flour, soda, salt, cinnamon and cloves; add raisins and walnuts to flour mixture. Add flour mixture to egg mixture; beat slightly. Bake at 350F in greased 13"x9"x2" pan. Check for doneness after 25 min.

Non-Sweet Frosting:
1 c. butter
5 T. flour
1 c. milk

1 c. powdered sugar
1 t. vanilla
1/2 c. broken walnuts

To make frosting, melt butter in saucepan; stir in flour until mixture bubbles. Add milk, stirring with wire whisk until mixture thickens. Cool. Add sugar and vanilla to cooked mixture; mix until smooth and blended. Spread on cooled cake; sprinkle with nuts. Yield: 12 servings.

Applesauce Bundt Coffee Cake

1 pkg. yellow cake mix   4 T. sugar
1-1/2 c. applesauce   2-1/2 T. cinnamon
3 eggs

Combine cake mix, applesauce and eggs, beat well. Grease bundt pan and sprinkle with some of the sugar and cinnamon. Pour in batter then cut in rest of sugar and cinnamon. Bake at 350F for 50 min. Let set 10 min., remove from pan and glaze with hot water and powdered sugar.

An apple is nature's toothbrush.

Apple Cake, Mom's

1/2 c. sugar   1 t. baking powder
1 T. butter   1 t. vanilla
1 egg   salt
1/3 c. milk   6 McIntosh apples
1 c. flour

Streusel: Mix until crumbly:
1/2 c. sugar   3/4 t. cinnamon
1 heaping T. flour   3/4 t. vanilla
1 T. butter

Cream butter and sugar; add egg, milk and vanilla. Stir well. Blend in flour, baking powder, and salt. Spread on 10"x14" greased cookie sheet. Peel and slice apples thin; arrange on dough in rows, completely covering. Sprinkle on streusel. Bake at 350F for 25-30 min. Delicious warm.

Apple Tart, Upside-Down

1/4 c. butter
1/3 c. brown sugar
1 T. light corn syrup
1 T. lemon juice

4 med. Haralson Apples
1 pie crust
1/2 t. cinnamon

Melt butter in 9" glass pie pan. Stir in sugar, corn syrup, lemon juice and cinnamon. Core apples, cut into slices. Arrange over brown sugar mixture in a circular pattern. Roll pie crust 1/4" thick. Drape over apples, tucking sides in around apples. Bake at 400F for 30-35 min., until crust is golden brown. Remove from oven, cool 5 min. Invert onto serving plate.

Apple-Carrot Cake

1-1/4 c. flour
1 t. baking soda
1 t. baking powder
1/2 t. cinnamon
1/2 t. salt
1/4 t. nutmeg
1/2 c. margarine

1 c. sugar
2 eggs
1 c. grated carrots
1/2 c. grated McIntosh apple
3 T. orange juice
1/2 c. nuts

Cream margarine and sugar; add eggs and beat well. Add carrots, apples and orange juice. Add dry ingredients and spices; mix well. Add nuts. Bake at 325F for 50 min. Sprinkle with powdered sugar or frost.

43

Apple Cake, German

3 eggs	2 c. flour
2 t. cinnamon	1 t. soda
1/2 t. salt	1 c. oil
1 t. vanilla	2 c. sugar
1/2 c. walnuts, chopped	4 c. Haralson apples, sliced

Frosting:

8 oz. cream cheese	1 t. vanilla
3 T. melted butter	1-1/2 c. powdered sugar

Mix all ingredients together with spoon (**do not use mixer**). Batter will be stiff. Spread into a greased and floured 9"x13" pan. Bake at 350F for 45-60 min. FROSTING: Mix and spread on cake or serve with whipped cream.

Oh! happy are the apples when the south winds blow.

Apple (Raw) Cake

4 c. sliced apples	] Add to
2 eggs	] apples and mix.
1/2 c. oil	] Mix together and
2 c. sugar	] add:
2 t. soda	2 t. cinnamon
2 c. flour	1 t. salt

Sift dry ingredients together and add to apple mixture and mix well. Bake at 350F for 40 min. Nuts may be added. When cool serve with Cool Whip or ice cream.

Applesauce Cake

4 eggs	2 t. soda
2 c. sugar	1 t. salt
1-1/2 c. oil	1 t. cinnamon
2 c. flour	1 c. applesauce

Beat eggs till thick; add everything but applesauce and mix well. Add applesauce and mix again. Pour into greased jellyroll pan and 9"x9" pan. Bake at 350F for 20 min.

Apple Cake, Low Cholesterol

3 c. chopped raw apple
3/4 c. sunflower oil
2 c. sugar
1 t. vanilla
2 egg whites

1 t. baking soda
2 c. flour
1 t. cinnamon
1 c. chiopped nuts

Mix all ingredients together; add some skim milk if dough is too stiff. Bake at 350F for 45-50 min. in 9"x13" pan.

Applesauce Cake

1/2 c. shortening
1/2 t. cinnamon
1/2 t. cloves
1/2 t. allspice
1 lg. egg
1-1/2 c. thick unsweetened
   applesauce

2-1/2 c. flour
1 c. raisins
1/2 c. chopped walnuts
2 t. soda
1/2 c. boiling water

Mix all together. Pour into well greased 9"x13" cake pan. Bake at 350F until toothpick inserted comes out clean. A powdered sugar frosting with 2 lg. T. peanut butter in the frosting is a must.

Applesauce Cake

1 c. sugar	2 t. soda
1/2 c. shortening	1 t. cinnamon
1 egg	1/4 t. cloves
1 c. sweetened applesauce	1 t. vanilla
1 c. nuts	pinch salt
2 c. flour	

Mix well in given order. Bake in loaf pan at 350F for approximately 1 hr.

Apple Crisp

3-4 Haralson apples	3/4 c. quick oatmeal
1 stick butter	1/2 c. flour
3/4 c. brown sugar	1 t. cinnamon

Slice apples into shallow baking dish. Melt butter in saucepan. Stir in brown sugar, oatmeal, flour amd cinnamon until crumbly; sprinkle over apples. Bake at 350F for 35 min. or until golden and apples are soft to fork. Serve with ice cream, whipped cream or cheese.

Apple Cake, Dutch

2 c. flour
1/2 c. oatmeal
3/4 c. melted butter
1 c. pkd brown sugar
1 t. salt
2 c. diced apples

1 c. water
1/4 t. salt
1 t. vanilla
1 c. sugar
3 T. cornstarch

Mix first 5 ingredients to crumb consistency. Save 1 c. for topping and spread the rest in 9"x13" cake pan. Put in apples. Mix together water, vanilla, salt, sugar and cornstarch and cook until thick. Pour over apples and bake at 350F for 45 min. Can be served warm or cold with whipped cream.

Gateau D'Eve (Eve's Cake)

1/2 c. flour
1/2 c. sugar
1 t. baking powder
1/2 c. milk

1/2 c. oil
7 apples
3 T. butter
1/2 c. sugar
1 egg

Peel apples and cut into slices. Mix the flour, 1/2 c. sugar, baking powder, milk and oil. Place the apples in a round quiche pan, and pour the above mixture over. Place in a 350F oven for 20 min. Remove from oven. Melt the butter, and mix with the egg and sugar. Mix together. Pour this mixture over the apple cake, and return to the oven for about 45 min.

Applesauce Cake, Chocolate

2 c. sifted flour	1/2 t. nutmeg
1-1/2 c. granulated sugar	2 eggs, unbeaten
1-1/2 t. salt	1/2 c. shortening
1-1/2 t. soda	2 c. applesauce
2 T. cocoa	1/2 c. walnuts, chopped
1/2 t. cinnamon	1/2 c. brown sugar
1/2 t. allspice	6 oz. pkg. chocolate chips
1/2 t. ground cloves	

Sift flour, sugar, salt, soda, cocoa and spices together; set aside. Beat eggs and shortening together in lg. mixing bowl. Add applesauce and sifted dry ingredients alternately to shortening mixture, mix well. Pour batter into a greased and floured 13"x9" cake pan. Combine walnuts, brown sugar and chocolate chips in a sm. bowl. Sprinkle over top of batter. Bake at 350F for 40 min.

CIDER

Hot Buttered Rum Cider

1 qt. fresh sweet apple
   cider
1/2 c. brown sugar

4 T. butter
2 cinnamon sticks
1 bottle (1/5) light rum

Combine cider, brown sugar and butter in saucepan. Heat, stirring until well mixed. Add cinnamon sticks (broken pieces) and simmer 20 min. Pour in rum, simmer 5-10 min. Do Not let mixture boil. Pour into mugs. Serve in front of a blazing fire with a platter of cheeses, sausage and apple wedges. Serves 12.

"He who flatters the cook never goes hungry."

Proverbs

Hot Mulled Cider

1/2 c. brown sugar
1/4 t. salt
2 qt. apple cider
1 t. whole allspice

1 t. whole cloves
3" stick cinnamon
dash of nutmeg
orange slices (opt)

Combine sugar, salt and cider. Tie spices in cheesecloth and add to cider. Slowly bring to a boil. Cover and simmer for 20 min. Remove spices. Serve hot with orange slice floaters. Use cinnamon sticks as stirrers if desired.

Apple Party Punch

2 c. natural sweet apple
  cider
1 c. orange juice, fresh or
  frozen
1/2 c. lemon juice, fresh or
  frozen

1 c. pineapple juice
2 c. cranberry juice
2 qt. chilled ginger ale
lemon and orange slices
fresh mint sprigs

Combine cider with the fruit juices and chill. At party time,
pour over a block of ice in a puch bowl. Add ginger ale and
stir. Float lemon and orange slices on top and garnish with
mint sprigs, opt.

Hot Juice/Cider

6 c. juice cider   **1/2 t. whole cloves**
1-2 sticks cinnamon

Heat in saucepan until simmer or perk in coffee pot putting spices in coffee pot basket.
Variations: Add a twist of lemon or add 1 (6 oz.) can of frozen lemonade concentrate or eliminate spices and add 1/8 c. red cinnamon candies.

Issac Newton is believed to thought up
the matter of gravity while
sitting under an apple tree.

Apple Juice Tea

Mix equal amounts of apple juice and strong tea. Pour over crushed ice. Garnish with mint leaves or lemon slices.

Other "Juicy" Ideas

Mix mayonnaise with equal parts apple juice. Good dressing for fruit, ham, chicken and turkey salads.

Use apple juice for the liquid in muffins, biscuits, small loaves of bread, rolls, pancakes and waffles.

Hot syrup for pancakes, waffles or french toast - thicken apple juice with cornstarch and mix with lemon juice for a hot syrup.

Apple Shake, Frosty

1 qt. apple juice, chilled
1 pt. vanilla ice cream,
   softened

1 (8-3/4 oz.) can crushed
   pineapple, opt.
1/2 t. cinnamon or sprinkle
   with nutmeg

Combine all ingredients in blender or with mixer until frothy.

Apple Toddy, Hot

1 qt. apple cider   1/2 lemon sliced
1/3 c. brown sugar   1/2 c. Southern Comfort

Simmer cider, sugar and lemon slices 10 min. Pour in Southern Comfort and serve in mugs.

Apple Brandy Brew

Combine and heat: 2 c. apple cider, 4/5 qt. applejack, 1 c. peach brandy and 1 cinnamon stick.

"A word fitly spoken is like apples gold,
in pictures of silver." Proverbs

Spicy Cider

Classification: easy	Preparation time: 2 min.
Planning: can prepare ahead	Servings: 4 to 6
	Cooking Time: 10-15 min.

4 c. apple cider or juice   orange slices or
1/4 c. red cinnamon candies   cinnamon sticks

Combine cider or juice and candies in a saucepan. Stir over med. heat until candies melt and cider is hot. Pour into mugs and garnish each with an orange slice or a cinnamon stick.

Mulled Cider

1 gal. apple cider   4 t. whole allspice
2 c. sugar   6 T. fresh lemon juice
48 whole cloves   1 c. fresh orange juice
12 cinnamon sticks   2-4 c. apple brandy

Combine all ingredients except apple brandy and bring to boil. Simmer 10 min.; add brandy. Strain and serve hot.

Apple Water

4 tart apples, peeled, cored and thinly sliced	scant 1/4 c. sugar peel of 1/2 a lemon 4 c. boiling water

Place apples and sugar in container with tight cover. With a vegetable peeler, remove outer yellow peel of lemon half. Add to apples, pour boiling water over all. Cover and let set aside and cool. When liquid has reached room temperature strain into a pitcher. Serve into frosty glasses with ice. Garnish with a lemon slice skewered on a straw. Makes 1 qt.

I often wished that all my causes were apple pie causes.

John Scott, Lord Eldon, referring to a complaint made to him when he was resident fellow of University College. Some of the undergraduates complained that the cooks had sent to table an apple-pie which could not be eaten. Lord Eldon ordered the cook to bring the pie before him, but the cook informed him that the pie was eaten, where-upon Lord Eldon, gave judgement for the defendant, saying to complainants:

"You complain that the pie could not be eaten,
but the pie has been eaten, and therefore could be eaten."

Hot Cider Syrup

1-1/2 c. apple cider   1/2 c. sugar
4" stick cinnamon broken   1/4 c. light corn syrup
1 t. whole cloves   2 T. butter or margarine

Combine cider, cinnamon and cloves in saucepan. Bring to boiling point, lower heat and simmer 10 min. Remove spice. Stir in sugar and corn syrup. Bring to boil again, cook 5 min. Remove from stove and stir in butter. Serve warm. Makes about 1-1/2 c. syrup.

DESSERTS

Apple Almond Crisp

6 apples, peel and sliced
1/2 c. white sugar
1/2 c. brown sugar
1 c. flour

1 t. cinnamon
1 c. chopped almonds
3/4 t. vanilla
1/2 c. melted butter

Combine dry ingredients; add butter and vanilla. Spread apples in a 9" round baking dish. Spoon flour mixture over apple slices to cover evenly. Bake at 400F for 30-40 min. Top with Half and Half, whipping cream or ice cream, however, just serving plain is great too.

Topping:
1 c. flour
3/4 c. brown sugar

6 T. butter
dash salt

Mix like pie crust; crumble on top. Bake 40-45 min at 375F.

Apple Crisp

2 c. flour
2 c. oatmeal
1 t. cinnamon
1/2 t. nutmeg

1-1/2 c. brown sugar
1-1/2 c. butter
2 qt. pared apple slices

Mix first 5 ingredients together and cut in butter until mixture is crumbly. Pat 1/2 of this mixture into a 9"x13" baking pan. Top with apples slices. Cover with remaining crumb mixture. Bake at 350F for 45-50 min., or until apples are tender and topping is browned.

Apple Crisp

Slice apples in a 9"x13" cake pan, 2/3 full with 1/2 c. of water, add 1 c. white sugar.

Topping:
1 c. flour	6 T. butter
3/4 c. brown sugar	dash salt

Mix like pie crust; crumble on top. Bake 40-45 min at 375F.

Apples, Baked

Wolf River apples	water
red cinnamon candies	marshmallows
butter	

Wash and core apples about 3/4 way to bottom. Fill hole about 1/2" from top with cinnamon candies. Top with a dab of butter. Place in baking dish. Add about 1/4"-1/2" water to pan. Cover and bake at 350F for 30 min. Remove cover and bake longer if necessary until tender. Put marshmallow in each apple and return to oven until melted.

Applesauce Donuts

2 eggs
1 c. sugar
3 T. shortening
1/2 c. milk
1 c. applesauce
2 t. baking powder

1 t. baking soda
1/2 t. salt
1/4 t. nutmeg
1/2 t. cinnamon
4 c. flour

Beat eggs, shortening and sugar. Stir in milk and apple-sauce. Blend in dry ingredients. Drop by t. into hot fat, about 375F. Fry till golden brown. When cool, shake in sugar, nutmeg and cinnamon mixture.

Apple Dumplings

1-1/2 c. water
1 c. sugar
4 Haralson apples,
    peeled and diced
1 c. flour

2 t. baking powder
1/2 t. salt
3 T. oleo
1/2 c. milk
cinnamon & sugar

Simmer 1-1/2 c. water and 1 c. sugar in 9"x9" pan for 5 min. Mix flour, baking powder, salt and oleo in lg. bowl; add apples and milk and stir well. Drop by spoonful into syrup. Sprinkle with cinnamon and sugar. Bake 425F for 30 min.

Apple Cobbler, Cinnamon

6 c. sliced tart apples	2 T. butter
1/4 t. salt	pastry (pie crust) to
1/2 t. cinnamon	cover the top
1/4 t. nutmeg	

Combine apples with sugar, salt and spices. Turn into 9" sq. pan or 8"x10" rectangle pan. Cover with pastry, cut gashes in the top. Bake in a very hot oven 450F for 10 min. Reduce heat to 350F and continue baking for 40 min. or until apples are done. Serve warm or cold with or without ice cream.

An Apple a day keeps the doctor away is a modern saying. However, the author and exact time some three hundred years ago in Devonshire, England are unknown, but they used to rhyme:
Written that a hobby a day keeps the doldrums away.

> "Ate an apfel avore gwain to bed,
> Makes the doctor beg his bread.

Apple Crisp

4 lg. tart apples	1/2 t. cinnamon
6 T. flour	1/4 t. mace
6 T. oatmeal	6 T. margarine
1/4 c. brown sugar	1 c. whipped topping

Pare and core apples; slice into a shallow 1 qt. baking dish. Combine dry ingredients and cut in margarine until mixture is crumbly. Sprinkle over apples. Bake in a 375F oven for 30 min. until apples are tender and top is browned. Serve with whipped topping. Yield: 6 servings.

Apple Duck Dessert

Preheat oven to 375F

2 c. flour   ] Mix and press
2 T. white sugar   ] in 9"x13"
2 sticks margarine   ] pan.

5 c. apples, peeled and sliced thin. Spread over bottom of crust. Sprinkle 3/4 c. sugar - 1 t. cinnamon on apples. Bake for 30 min.

Prepare Pudding: 1 lg. instant vanilla pudding, let set till firm and pour over hot baked apples, cool and cover with Cool Whip then refrigerate.

Applescotch Dessert

1-1/4 c. brown sugar
1 T. cornstarch
1-1/2 t. vanilla
1/8 t. salt
1/4 c. butter or margarine
2 c. flour
1/4 c. white sugar

1 T. baking powder
1/3 c. shortening
3 c. chopped, peeled tart
   apples
3/4 c. milk
1 T. white sugar
1/2 t. cinnamon

In a lg. saucepan: Mix brown sugar, cornstarch, and salt. Add 2 c. cold water; cook until bubbly. Cook and stir 2 min. more. Add 1 t. vanilla and 2 T. butter. Pour into 13"x9"x2" baking dish. Combine flour, and 1/4 c. white sugar, baking powder, and 1/2 t. salt. Cut in shortening. Stir in apple. Stir in milk and remaining vanilla till moistened. Drop by T. over syrup. Combine the 1 T. white sugar and cinnamon; sprinkle on top. Dot with remaining butter. Bake in 350F oven for 50 min. Serves 10.

Almond Apples

4 apples, peel and cored to
    about 1/2" from bottom,
    leaving bottom intact
2 T. + 2 t. margarine, melt
4 zwiiback, made into fine
    crumbs
1/4 c. raisins
1 oz. almonds toasted and
    chopped *
2 t. sugar
1/4 t. cinnamon
1/8 t. almonds extract

Spray a 2 qt. shallow casserole with nonstick cooking spray. Dip apples into margarine, then into crumbs, reserving remaining margarine; stand apples upright in casserole. Preheat oven to 350F. In sm. bowl combine remaining margarine with raisins, almonds, sugar, cinnamon and extract; mixing well. Fill cavity of each apple with 1/4 of raisin mixture. Bake uncovered for 40 min.; cover and bake about 10 min. longer or until apples are tender.
* To toast almonds, place on baking sheet and bake at 350F for 5-10 min., shaking baking sheet occasionally.

Apple Cobbler

7 tart apples
2 T. lemon juice
3/4 c. sugar
1/2 t. cinnamon
1/2 t. nutmeg
3 T. butter
2 T. brown sugar
4 T. butter
1 c. flour
1-1/2 t. baking powder
1/2 t. salt
1/3 c. milk

Pare, core and slice the apples. Combine apples, spices, sugar and lemon juice. Place in an 8" baking dish and dot with 3 T. butter. Mix flour, baking powder and salt in a bowl; stir in brown sugar and cut in butter until mixture is crumbly. Stir in milk, mixing until dough forms a ball. Pat over apples in pan. Brush top with milk and sprinkle with sugar and cinnamon. Bake at 350F until apples are tender and crust is lightly browned. Serve with Half and Half poured over servings.

The apple is the oldest and
most widely grown fruit,
but it is a member of the rose family.

Apple Bread Pudding, Golden

8 slices bread	1/2 c. sugar
3-4 Cortland apples, divided	1/2 t. cinnamon
1/2 c. golden raisins	1/4 t. nutmeg
1-1/3 c. milk	1/4 t. salt
1/4 c. butter or margarine	1/4 c. pkd. brown sugar
5 eggs, beaten	dairy sour cream (Opt)

Toast bread lightly and cut diagonally into fourths. Arrange a single layer of bread in botton of layered 12"x8"x2" baking dish. Core and slice 1 apple. Core and slice remaining apples to = 4 c. Spread diced apples evenly on bread. Sprinkle raisins over apples. Arrange remaining bread in 2 lengthwise rows on diced apples. Place apple slices between rows of bread. Heat milk and butter only until butter melts. Combine beaten eggs, sugar and seasonings. Gradually add milk mixture, stirring constantly. Pour over bread and apples. Sprinkle with brown sugar. Bake uncovered at 350F for 40-50 min. or until a thin knife blade inserted near center comes out clean. Serve warm or cold. Top with sour cream. Makes 8-10 servings.

Apples, Fried

8 sliced apples	1 t. cinnamon
3 T. butter	1 t. nutmeg
1 or 2 T. sugar	

Melt butter in frypan. Add unpeeled apple slices. Stir and fry apples till soft; add sugar, cinnamon and nutmeg, to taste. Serve as a side dish, hot or cold, or as a dessert.

Apple Crumble

5 or 6 apples, pared and sliced (about 3c.)	3 T. flour
	3/4 c. quick cooking oats
1/3 c. water	1/2 c. brown sugar
2 T. lemon juice	1/3 c. peanut butter
3/4 t. cinnamon	2 T. butter

Arrange sliced apples in baking dish. Sprinkle with water, lemon juice and cinnamon. Combine remaining ingredients; mix well. Spread on apples. Bake at 300F for about 50 min.

Apple Dumplings Deluxe

1 beaten egg
1 8-oz. sour cream
2 c. flour
2 T. sugar
1/4 t. baking soda
2 t. baking powder
1/4 t. salt
4 c. thinly sliced, peeled
   apples
1/4 c. sugar

1/2 t. cinnamon
1/4 t. nutmeg
1-1/2 c. water
1-1/4 c. pkd brown sugar
1 c. sugar
2 T. cornstarch
2 T. lemon juice
2 T. butter or margarine
(Opt) Light cream OR
   ice cream

1) For dough: In a med. mixing bowl combine egg and sour cream. In a sm. mixing bowl stir together flour, the 2 T. sugar, baking powder, baking soda and salt; add to sour cream mixture. Mix well.

2) On a lightly floured surface roll dough to a 12" sq. Spread apples on top. In a sm. bowl combine the 1/4 c. sugar, cinnamon and nutmeg; sprinkle on top of apples. Carefully roll up dough. Cut into 12-1" thick slices.

3) Place slices, cut side down, in a greased 13"x9"x2" baking pan. Stir together water, brown sugar, the 1 c. sugar, cornstarch, and lemon juice; pour over slices in pan. Dot with butter or margarine.

4) Bake uncovered in a 350F oven for 35-40 min. or until golden brown. To serve, spoon warm dumplings and juices into individual dessert dishes. Serve with cream or ice cream. 12 servings.

Apples, Baked

Classification: easy　　　　Preparation time: 10 min.
Planning: can perpare ahead　Servings: 4
　　　　　　　　　　　　　　Baking time: 40 min.

4 apples, washed, cored　　16 raisins
1/4 c. pkd. brown sugar　　1/2 t. cinnamon
4 t. butter

Preheat oven to 350F. Place apples in a pie plate. Combine remaining ingredients and spoon evenly into center of each apple. Sprinkle any extra filling over the top. Bake 40 min. or until apples are tender. Baste with juices from the pie plate. Serve hot with a scoop of ice cream or a dollop of whipped cream.

Pudding, Apple

1 c. sugar　　　　　　　1/2 c. butter
1/4 c. butter　　　　　　1 c. flour
1 beaten egg　　　　　　1 t. baking soda
2 c. apples, chopped　　　1/2 t. cinnamon

Sauce:
1/4 c. butter　　　　　　1/2 c. brown sugar
1/2 c. cream　　　　　　1/2 c. white sugar
1/2 t. vanilla

Cream together sugar and butter; add beaten egg. Add apples and nuts. Add flour, soda and cinnamon. Blend well and pour into buttered and floured 8"x8" pan. Bake at 350F for 30 min.
Sauce: Mix all ingredients. Boil 5 min. and serve warm on pudding.

69

Apple Crisp

8 med. apples   1 c. oatmeal
 (Wealthies or Greenings) 2 t. cinnamon
1-1/2 c. pkd. brown sugar 1 t. nutmeg
1 c. flour   2/3 c. soft butter

Grease a 9"x13" cake pan. Peel, core and slice apples.
Place in cake pan. Mix/cut in brown sugar, flour, oatmeal,
cinnamon, nutmeg, and butter in med. size bowl. (Mixture
will be crumbly.) Sprinkle over apples and bake at 350F for
30-35 min. or until apples are tender. Yields 8-12 servings.
Cool and serve with ice cream or whipped cream. To make
an 8"x8" pan, just 1/2 ingredients. Baking time would be the
same.

One rotten apple in the barrel is enough to spoil all the rest.

Apple Pudding

1 c. granulated sugar   1/2 t. cinnamon
1/2 c. margarine   1/4 t. salt
1 egg   1 t. vanilla
1 c. flour   4 cooking apples
1 t. soda   (McIntosh/Greening) do
1/4 t. nutmeg   not chop too fine

Cream sugar and shortening; add egg. Add the rest of the
ingredients and mix well. Put into 8"x8" pan and bake at
350F for 45 min.

Apple Jack

2-1/2 c. flour
1 t. salt

1 c. shortening
1 egg yolk, + milk to make
   2/3 c.

Filling:
8-10 wealthy or McIntosh
   apples, peel and sliced
1 c. sugar

2 handfuls crushed cornflakes
1 egg white whipped with fork

Glaze: or
1 c. powdered sugar
1 T. water
1 t. vanilla

Glaze:
1 c. powdered sugar
1 T. butter
2 T. warm milk
1/4 t. almond flavoring

Mix crust in order given; divide dough into two parts. Roll out one part to fill a 9"x13" pan. Sprinkle crust with crushed cornflakes. Arrange apples evenly over curst; sprinkle with cinnamon and sugar. Roll out remaining crust, place on top of apples. Pinch edges. Brush top crust with beaten egg white. Bake at 350F for 1 hr. Remove from oven and frost with glaze while warm. Serve warm with a fork or cool and cut into bars. Serves 10-12. This keeps well.

Apple Pudding

1 c. sugar   milk
1 c. flour   cinnamon
3 t. baking powder 2 T. butter
1/4 t. salt

Put sliced apples on bottom of dish. Mix above ingredients with milk enough to pour over apples. The batter should be consistency of pancake batter. Top with butter and cinnamon. Bake at 350F for 1 hr.

Apple Fritters

1 beaten egg   3 T. apple cider
1 c. milk   1/2 t. vanilla
1 c. finely chopped apple 2 c. flour
1/4 c. sugar   1 T. baking powder
1/4 t. salt   powdered sugar

Combine and mix egg, milk, apple, sugar, salt, cider, and vanilla. Stir together flour and baking powder; fold into egg mixture, stirring just until all flour is moistened. Drop batter by rounded t. into hot oil 350F. Fry until golden brown, turning once, about 3-4 Min. Drain well on paper towels. Roll in sugar or powdered sugar. Makes 40.

Apple Bread Pudding

4 c. soft bread crumbs,
    crusts trimmed
1 c. diced apples, peeled
2 c. scalded milk
2 T. butter, melted
3 eggs
1/2 c. sugar OR 1/3 c. Honey

1 t. vanilla
1 t. cinnamon
1/4 t. nutmeg
1/4 t. cloves
1 t. grated lemon rind

Mix bread (white, whole wheat or combination) with apples; set aside. Combine milk, butter, eggs, honey/sugar, vanilla, cinnamon, nutmeg, cloves and lemon rind in blender or with hand mixer. Pour over apple, bread mixture. Pour into a buttered 2 qt. casserole. Set dish in a larger pan of hot water; bake at 350F for 1 hr. or until knife inserted in center comes out clean. Serve warm with whipped cream or ice cream. Yield: 6 servings.
* Diabetic Exchanges: 1 serving = 1 fruit, 1 bread, 3/4 milk, 2 fats; also, 281 calories, 271 mg. sodium, 149 mg. cholesterol, 38 gm. carbohydrate, 9 gm. protein, 11 gm. fat.

With a heart that is true,
I'll be waiting for you,
In the shade of the old apple tree.

Apple Cobbler for Two

3 T. brown sugar
1/4 t. ground cinnamon
1/4 t. ground nutmeg
1 t. lemon juice
2 med. size cooking apples, peeled and sliced

1/3 c. all-purpose flour
2 T. sugar
1 t. baking powder
2 T. milk
1 T. vegetable oil

Combine 3 T. brown sugar, cinnamon, nutmeg and lemon juice; add apples, and toss well to coat. Spoon apple mixture into two 10 oz. custard cups. Set aside.

Combine flour, 2 T. sugar, and baking powder in a sm. bowl. Combine milk and oil; stir into flour mixture until moistened. Drop dough by t. onto apple mixture. Bake at 375F for 15-20 min. Serve warm. Yield: 2 servings.

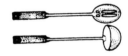

Apple Torte, Bavarian

1/2 c. butter
1/3 c. sugar
1/2 t. vanilla
1 c. flour
1 8-oz. pkg. cream cheese
1/4 c. sugar

1 egg
1/2 t. vanilla
1/3 c. sugar
1/2 t. cinnamon
4 apples, sliced
1/4 c. sliced almonds

Preheat oven to 450F. Cream butter, sugar and vanilla. Stir in flour to form dough. Press dough onto bottom and sides of a 9" spring form pan. Combine cheese, sugar, egg and vanilla. Pour onto crust. Toss apples with sugar and cinnamon. Arrange on cream cheese. Sprinkle with nuts. Bake 10 min. Reduce heat to 400F and bake 25 min. Cool slightly before removing from pan.

Apple Cheese Crisp

1/4 c. + 1 T. butter or margarine	3 T. flour, divided
1/2 c. brown sugar	1/2 t. cinnamon
3/4 c. oatmeal	1/4 t. salt
3/4 c. flour	3 or 4 oz. cream cheese - room temperature
6 c. sliced pared apples	1 T. milk
1 T. lemon juice	1/4 c. white sugar
1/3 c. white sugar	1 egg

Microwave butter in casserole for 45-60 sec., or until melted. Stir in brown sugar and oats. Microwave on high for 2 min. Stir in 3/4 c. flour; set aside. Combine apples, lemon juice, 1/3 c. sugar, 2 T. flour, cinnamon and salt in 8"x8" baking dish. Stir and spread evenly. Microwave on high for 8 min., stirring after 4 min. Blend cream cheese, milk, sugar, egg and 1 T. flour. Pour evenly over apples. Sprinkle with cumbly mixture. Microwave on high 6-10 min., rotating a half-turn after 3-5 min. Serve warm or cold, plain or topped.

75

Apple Slump

6 c. pared, cored, sliced
   apples
1 c. brown sugar
1 t. cinnamon
1 t. nutmeg
1/2 c. water

pinch salt
1-1/4 c. flour
1/4 t. salt
1 t. baking powder
3/4 c. milk

Place apples into a 3 qt. saucepan; add sugar, spices, salt and water. Stir to mix; cook over low heat until mushy but not dry. Meanwhile, mix flour, salt and baking powder in a med. bowl. Stir in enough milk to make a soft dough. Drop by sm. T. of dough into hot applesauce. Cover and cook over low heat for about 20 min., or until the slump tests done. (Center is not doughy when pierced with a knife) Serve in sauce dishes, with cream or whipped topping.

Apple Tart, Autumn

1-1/2 c. flour
5 t. sugar
1/4 t. salt
1 t. grated lemon zest
6 T. unsalted butter
6 T. solid veg. shortening

3 T. ice water
1 t. vanilla
2 Haralson apples
3 T. melted unsalted butter
1 T. sugar
1/8 t. cinnamon

Combine flour, sugar, salt and lemon zest. Cut 6 T. butter and shortening into sm. pieces and add to dry ingredients; cut into flour until it resembles coarse meal. Add ice water 1 T. at a time, add vanilla. With hands, mix until gathered in a ball. Flatten slightly, cover with plastic wrap and chill 1 hr. Grease and flour baking sheet. On waxed paper roll out to 1/8" thickness. Cut out 6 circles 4" diameter and place on baking sheet. Peel apples and slice thin. Arrange in spiral pattern, overlapping slightly on crust. Brush with melted butter and bake 375F for 20 min. Remove from oven, brush again and sprinkle with sugar and cinnamon (mixed). Return to oven 10 min. carefully remove to cool on rack.

Apple/Cranberry Crisp

3 c. chopped apples,   2 c. raw cranberries
   unpeeled   3/4 -1 c. granulated sugar

Topping:
1-1/2 c. old fashioned OR   1/3 c. flour
   quick cooking oats   1/3 c. chopped pecans
1/2 c. pkd. brown sugar   1/2 c. melted butter

Combine apples, cranberries and sugar in 8" sq. baking dish or 2 qt. casserole; mix thoroughly to blend; set aside. Combine topping ingredients until crumbly; spread evenly over fruit layer. Bake at 350F for 1 hr. or until fruit is fork tender. Serve warm with ice cream or whipped cream. Yield: 8 servings.

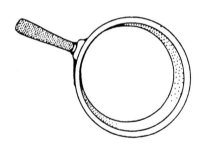

In 1937 the most popular jazz dance was the big apple.

Apples, Skillet Buttery

1/2 c. butter   1-1/2 c. water
1/2 c. sugar   1/2 t. cinnamon
2 T. cornstarch, heaping   4 McIntosh apples

Cut apples in half and core; **do not peel.** Melt butter in skillet and stir in sugar, cornstarch, water and cinnamon. Lay apples cut side down in mixture; cover skillet, cook on med. heat until tender, about 20-25 min.

Apple Pizza Pie

Crust:
1-1/4 c. flour
1 t. salt
1/2 c. shortening

1/4 c. cold milk
7 c. sliced tart apples

Topping:
1/4 c. butter
1/2 c. brown sugar
1/2 c. white sugar
1/3 c. flour

1/4 t. salt
1 t. cinnamon
1/2 t. nutmeg

For crust, mix and then roll ingredients to fit a 10" pizza pan.
Sprinkle crust with parmesan cheese. Set crust aside while
preparing the topping. Mix all topping ingredients. Sprinkle
1/2 of the topping mixture on the crust. Cover with apple
slices, overlapping slightly. Sprinkle with 2 T. lemon juice.
Add 1/4 c. butter to rest of topping mixture and sprinkle over
apple slices/crust. Bake at 400F for 30 min. Cut into
wedges to serve.

Apple Dessert, Dutch

5 med. apples, pare, core
   and sliced (about 5 c.)
1 14-oz. can sweetened
   condensed milk
1 t. cinnamon

1/2 c. + 2 T. cold margarine
1-1/2 c. biscuit baking mix
1/2 c. brown sugar
1/2 c. chopped nuts

Preheat oven to 325F. In med. bowl, combine apples, sweetened condensed milk and cinnamon. In a lg. bowl, cut 1/2 c. margarine into 1 c. of biscuit mix until crumbly. Stir in apple mixture. Pour into greased 9" sq. baking pan. In a sm. bowl, combine remaining 1/2 c. biscuit mix and sugar; cut in remaining 2 T. margarine until crumbly. Add nuts. Sprinkle evenly over apple mixture. Bake 1 hr. or until golden. Serve warm with ice cream if desired.

Apple Crisp, Individual

2/3 c. pared and sliced
   apples
1/8 c. brown sugar
1/8 t. nutmeg
1/4 c. flour

2 t. water
1/8 c. sugar
dash salt
1/8 t. cinnamon
1/8 c. butter

Place 1/2 the apple and 1 t. water in each of two custard cups. Combine sugars, salt, spices and flour in a bowl. Cut in butter with pastry blender. Sprinkle crumb mix in each custard cup. Place cups on cookie sheets and bake in a preheated oven at 375F about 25 min.

Apple Crisp w/Orange Juice

4 c. pared and sliced tart
   apples
1/4 c. orange juice
1 c. sugar
3/4 c. flour

1 t cinnamon
1/4 t. nutmeg
dash salt
1/3 c. butter

Place apples in a buttered pie plate and pour the orange juice over them. Combine sugar, flour, spices and salt; cut in butter until mixture is crumbly. Sprinkle over apples. Bake at 375F for 45 min. or until apples are tender and topping is browned and crisp. Serve warm with cream. Makes 4-6 servings.

Apple Krumble Pizza

2 pie crusts (line bottom
   of pizza pan)
6 or 7 apples

1/2 c. sugar
1 t. cinnamon
1/4 t. nutmeg

Sprinkle on Top:
3/4 c. flour
1/2 c. sugar

1/2 c. butter

Arrange sliced apples on crusts in pizza pan. Mix together sugar, cinnamon and nutmeg; sprinkle on top of sliced apples. Next sprinkle on top the combination of flour, sugar and butter. Bake at 450F (center of oven) for 30-40 min.

MAIN DISHES

Apple & Sauerkraut, Pork Chops

1 T. + 1 t. margarine	2 t. Dijon style mustard
1 apple, cored and sliced	1/2 t. caraway seed
1/4 c. sliced onion	1/8 t. pepper
3/4 c. drained sauerkraut	2 pork loin chops (6 oz. each
1/4 c. chicken broth	and 1/2" thick)
1 T. + 1 t. dry white wine	

Heat margarine, add apple and onion; saute 2-3 min. Remove from skillet and set aside. To skillet add sauerkraut and sauté, stirring occasionally until liquid is evaporated 2-3 min. Add broth, wine, mustard, caraway seed, and pepper; mix well. Reduce heat to low, cover and let simmer, stirring occasionally, for 8-10 min. While mixture is simmering, broil chops on rack in broiler pan 4"-6 " from heat, turning once about 4-6 min. on each side. Add chops and reserved apple mixture to skillet and let simmer about 2 min. Remove chops to serving plate and surround with sauerkraut mixture.

In Ireland, the apple tree
is believed to represent immortality.

Apples, Pork Chop w/Cabbage

4 pork chops, cut 3/4" thick
   (1 1-1/4 lbs)
1/2 c. water
1/2 of sm. head red or
   green cabbage,
   shredded (3 c.)
2 T. vinegar

1 T. Dijon style mustard
1-1/2 t. sugar
1/8 t. salt
1/8 t. caraway seed
2 apples, cored and cut into
   thin wedges
1/3 c. raisins

Trim excess fat from chops. Place chops on unheated broiler pan rack. Broil 5" from heat 20 to 25 min. or till no longer pink, turning once. In a large saucepan bring water to boiling. Add cabbage, cook, uncovered, about 3 min. or till almost tender. Drain; return to saucepan. In bowl gradually combine vinegar and mustard. Stir in sugar, salt, caraway seed and dash pepper. Add apples and raisins; toss to coat. Add to cabbage; toss to mix. Cover and cook 2 to 3 min. or until apples are crisp-tender and mixture is heated through. Serve chops over cabbage and apple mixture. Serves 4. 214 calories per serving.

Apple Pork Chops

1 T. oil
4 pork chops, about
   1" thick
1 can condensed chicken
   broth (10-3/4 oz.)
2 T. soy sauce
1 T. vinegar
1/2 c. apple cider

2 T. brown sugar
2 T. cornstarch
1/2 t. ground ginger
1 lg. apple, cored and
   coarsely chopped
cooked rice
sliced green onions

In a 10" skillet, heat oil over med.-high. Brown chops on both sides. Stir in chicken broth, soysauce and vinegar; bring to a boil. Reduce heat, cover and simmer 20 min. or until chops are tender. Meanwhile, in a sm. bowl, combine cider, brown sugar, cornstarch and ginger; stir until

smooth. Remove chops from skillet and keep warm. Increase heat to med. Stir cornstarch mixture into skillet; cook and stir until thickened. Add chopped apple and heat through. On a platter, arrange chops over rice. Spoon sauce over chops and top with chopped green onions. Serves 4.

Apple Onion Casserole, Sausage

6 med. onions, sliced
8 med. apples, sliced and
   peeled

2 lbs. sausage
2/3 c. brown sugar
4 T. orange juice

Cook onions in salted water for 5 min; drain. Cook sausage and drain. In a 2 qt. greased casserole put layer of onions, apple and sausage. Sprinkle 1/3 of brown sugar. Then another layer of onion, apple and sausage and 1/3 c. brown sugar. Pour the orange juice over the top. Bake at 350F for 20 min. covered, 15 min. uncovered.

Apples and Sweet Potatoes

1/2 c. bread crumbs or
   cracker crumbs
3 T. butter, melted
1/3 c. brown sugar
3/4 t. cinnamon

1-1/2 c. thin sliced sweet
   potatoes
1-1/2 c. chopped apples,
   peeled
1 t. lemon juice
3 T. water

Stir bread crumbs into butter; add sugar salt and spices. Place half the mixture in a greased casserole. Add half the sweet potatoes, then half the apples. Combine lemon juice with water; sprinkle half on apples and potatoes. Repeat layers, ending with the crumb mixture. Cover and bake in 350F oven for 45 min. Uncover and brown lightly. Makes 6 servings.

Pork Chops w/Vegetable, Cider

1/2 t. thyme	2 med. onions, quartered
1/2 t. salt	2 med. potatoe cut 3/4" cube
1/2 t. pepper	2 lg. carrots cut 1"
4 pork chops 1" thick	1 turnip, peeled and cubed
1 T. olive oil	3/4 c. cream
2 c. apple cider	2 T. flour
1/4 c. dry sherry	1/4 t. nutmeg

Combine thyme, salt and pepper, rub into trimmed chops. In a 12" skillet brown chops in oil over med. heat 4 min. per side. Remove chops. Add cider and sherry to skillet. Return chops; add vegetables. Reduce heat; simmer, covered 45 min. Remove chops and vegetables to platter. Keep warm. Boil remaining liquid uncovered about 8 min. For gravy, in bowl slowly stir cream into flour and nutmeg; add to liquid, stirring constantly. Cook and stir until bubbly. Cook 1 min. more.

She is lost with an apple, and won with a nut.
He that is won with a nut may be lost with an apple.

Apple Quiche

1/2 lb. bulk Italian sausage	1 T. sugar
1/2 c. chopped onion	1/2 c. shredded cheddar
1-1/2 c. apples, pared, cored	cheese
cut into 1/2" cubes	4 eggs, beaten
1 T. lemon or lime juice	2 c. light cream or milk
	Pastry for single 9" pie crust

In a large skillet, cook sausage and onion until sausage is browned and onion is tender; about 10 min. stirring frequently. Remove from heat and drain off excess fat.

In a bowl, toss apples with lemon or lime juice and the sugar. Add sausage mixture, cheese, eggs and cream; mix well.

Line a 9" quiche dish or pie plate with pastry. Turn apple mixture into dish. Bake in a 350F oven 40-50 min. or until custard is set. Let stand 10 min. before cutting to serve. Makes 6 serings.

Apples, Scalloped

2 c. stale bread crumbs,
   preferably French or
   homemade bread
2 T. melted butter
3 c. pared, chopped apples
1/2 c. sugar

1 T. grated lemon peel
1/4 t. cinnamon
1/4 t. nutmeg
1/4 c. water
2 T. lemon juice

Combine bread crumbs and butter. Sprinkle 1/4 over bottom of greased 8"x8" baking pan. Top with half of the apples. Combine sugar, lemon peel and spices; sprinkle half over the apples. Repeat layers: crumbs, apples, spices. Mix water and lemon juice, drizzle over apples. Top with remaining crumbs. Cover pan with foil and bake at 375F for 45 min. uncover and bake 15 min. more, or until crumbs are browned. Makes 6 servings.

Apple-Sausage Stuffing

1 lb. pork sausage
1 lg. onion, chopped
1 c. celery, chopped
1/2 lb. sliced mushrooms
2 apples pared and
   chopped
1 c. fresh parsley, chopped

1 t. sage
1 t. thyme
1 lb. French or homemade
   bread, cut into 1" cubes
2 c. chicken broth
salt and pepper to taste

Brown sausage in skillet, breaking up lumps. Drain off grease. Add onion and celery, saute 10 min. add apples, mushrooms, parsley and herbs; saute 10 more min. Mix with remaining ingredients, season to taste with salt and pepper. Chill completely before stuffing a turkey, or put into a casserole and bake 1 hr. at 350F.

Apple Stuffing

1 loaf (1 lb) day-old white
   bread, cut into 1/2"
   cubes
1/3 c. butter
1/2 c. chopped onion
1/2 c. chopped celery
1/4 c. chopped celery
   leaves

2 T. chopped parsley
1/4 t. salt
1/8 t. pepper
2 c. milk
2 eggs, lightly beaten
2 apples, pared, cored and
   chopped (3 c.)
1/4 c. raisins

Preheat oven to 375F. Place bread cubes on cookie sheet. Bake bread cubes in preheated oven until dry and lightly toasted, about 5 min.; transfer to a large bowl. Lower oven temperature to 350F. Combine gently rest of ingredients in bowl and place in a greased 6 c. baking dish. Bake at 350F for 1 hr. Serve with any meat - especially turkey, chicken or pork.

Apple Meat Loaf

2-1/2 lbs. lean hamburger
1-1/2 c. pkg. stuffing mix
2 c. fine chopped tart apples
   apples
3 eggs

2 t. salt
2 T. prepared mustard
1 lg. onion, minced
3 T. prepared horseradish
3/4 c. ketchup

Combine ingredients, mix thoroughly and pack into greased 8"x5"x3" loaf pan. Bake at 350F for 1 hr.

Apple-Sausage Dressing

1 lb. pork sausage
1 med. onion, chopped
1 c. celery, sliced
1/2 c. margarine or sun-
   flower oil
2 t. parsley flakes
1/2 t. salt

1/2 t. sage
1/2 t. sweet basil
2 c. apples, chopped
apple cider as needed
8 oz. pkg. croutons or
   bread cubes

Crumble sausage and brown lightly in lg. pan, drain off most of the grease. Add all other ingredients, except cider and bread cubes, while heating on med.; mix thoroughly. Add bread and mix again; add enough cider to moisten as you wish.

The United States Department of Agriculture
lists 7,000 varieties of apples grown in the U.S.,
however 13 varieties provide over 90% of
the total apple crop.

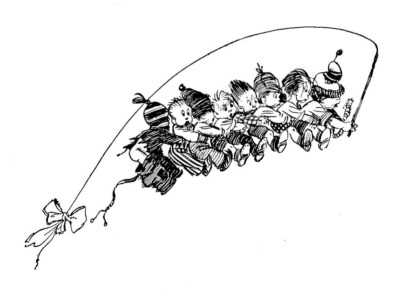

Apple Sauce Chicken Bake

2 c. applesauce,   dash of pepper
   unsweetened   bread crumbs
3/4 t. seasoned salt   cut up chicken

Mix applesauce, salt and pepper. Dip chicken pieces in mixture. Roll in crumbs. Bake about 1 hr. at 350F. This is a low Cholesterol recipe.

Apple, Fried Potatoe w/Bacon

8 slices bacon, diced   1/2 t. salt
3 lg. poatoes, sliced 1/4"   1/4 t. pepper
2/3 c. onion, chopped   3 lg. McIntosh apples, cored
1/4 c. cider vinegar   and cut in wedges

Fry bacon over med. heat until crisp; drain and put aside. Add potatoes, onion, vinegar, salt and pepper to pan. Cover and cook over med. heat, stirring occasionally, 20-25 min. Add apples and bacon during last 5 min.

Apple and Bacon, Sautéd

8 slices bacon
2 T. brown sugar

4 c. tart apples, pared, cored
and cubed

In a frying pan, sauté bacon until crisp. Remove and drain, reserving 2 T. fat. Sauté apples in bacon fat until translucent. Sprinkle with sugar. Arrange apples on a platter surrounded by the bacon. Serves 4-6.

Apple Sausage Bake

8 pork sausage
6 tart apples, cored & sliced

1/2 c. brown sugar

Brown the sausages in a skillet and place in a baking dish. Arrange apples around sausage and sprinkle with sugar. Bake at 400F for 10 min. Reduce heat to 350F and bake another 15 min.

Apples, Egg Casserole

4 cooking apples, peeled
   and thinly sliced
2 T. sugar
1 lb. fried bacon, crumbled

8 oz. pkg. shredded sharp
   cheddar cheese
4 eggs, beaten
1-1/2 c. biscuit mix
1-1/2 c. milk

Preheat oven to 375F. Mix apples and sugar; spread evenly in bottom of greased 9"x13" pan. Sprinkle cheese and bacon over this. Beat eggs until frothy; add biscuit mix and milk. Pour over cheese and bacon in pan. Bake for 35 min. or until golden brown. Serves 8-9.

Apple Cider, Bratwurst

1 pkg. uncooked bratwurst
12 oz. apple cider
4 whole cloves
1 apple, cored, thinly sliced

1 T. yellow mustard
1/4 c. Half & Half
salt & pepper to taste

In frying pan, bring apple cider to a boil. Pierce brats and add to cider along with cloves. Simmer for 10 min.; add apple. Cover and simmer another 10 min.; remove apple slices and brats. Simmer cider mixture until reduced by half; add mustard, Half & Half, salt and pepper. Return brats to fry pan and heat for another 5 min. Serve with cider sauce.

The apples lie scattered here and there, each
under its own tree. (Strata jacent passim sua
quaeque sub arbore poma.)

Old Fortune, like sly Farmer Dapple,
Where there's an orchard, flings an apple.

Apples-Chestnuts, Pheasant

1 Pheasant, about
    3-1/2 lbs.
1/2 c. butter
salt
ground pepper
1/2 t. rosemary

6 apples, peeled and
    quartered
1 can chestnuts (whole 1 lb.
    5 oz.)
1/2 c. port wine

Rub cavity of pheasant with salt, pepper and crushed
rosemary. Melt 4 T. butter in skillet and brown pheasant on
all sides, turning frequently. Heat remaining butter in large,
heavy casserole or Dutch oven; add apples and cook for 5
min. Add chestnuts; place on top, cover tightly and cook in
preheated 550F oven for 25 min. Remove from oven and stir
in port wine. Allow bird to rest in casserole 20 min. longer.
Serve pheasant on large platter surrounded by the apple-
chestnut garnish and serve with wild or brown rice and the
sauce. The Hunters Delight!!

Acorn Squash, Apple Stuffed

3 acorn squash, cut in half   1 c. nuts, chopped
4-5 Med. red apples, cored   3/4 c. maple syrup
    and diced   1/2 c. butter, melted

Clear out insides of squash and place in baking dish filled with 1/2" water. Combine apples, nuts, maple syrup, and all but 2T. butter and fill center cavity of squash with this mixture. Use remaining 2 T. butter to brush surfaces of squash. Cover pan with aluminum foil and bake at 400F for 45 min.

Apples, Pork Chops with

Tart cooking apples are traditionally served with pork to counteract the fattiness of the meat. They appear as stuffings and sauces with roasts, and can also, as here, be used with oven-cooked chops.

PREPARATION TIME: 15 min.
COOKING TIME: 1 hr. 10 min.

4 thick pork chops	3-4 lg cooking apples
2-4 T. unsalted butter	juice of 1 lemon
salt & black pepper	

Trim any excess fat from the chops and put them in a buttered oven-proof dish. Season to taste with salt and freshly ground pepper. Peel, core, and thinly slice the apples, and arrange over the chops to cover them completely. Melt the remaining butter and brush some of it over the apple slices. Sprinkle with lemon juice and cover the dish tightly with a lid or foil.

Cook the chops in the center of a preheated oven at 325F for 1 hr. Remove the foil, brush the apples with the remaining butter, and cook for a further 10 min., or until the apples are lightly browned but not dry, and the chops are tender. Serve the chops from the cooking dish or on a warmed serving plate. Small new potatoes and braised Belgian endive go well with the sharp apple taste.

Applesauce Pork Chop

2 c. applesauce	1/8 t. garlic salt
1 t. horseradish	4 pork chops 1", trimmed

Trim fat from pork chops and place in baking dish. Combine rest of ingredients and cover the chops. Bake at 325F. for 1 hr.

Apple Pot Roast

pot roast
1/2 c. water
2 beef bouillon cubes
1/4 t. garlic powder
1 sm. bay leaf

1/8 t. thyme
1 c. applesauce
6 carrots, sliced
1 onion, sliced
1 apple, sliced

Brown roast in lg. pot; add next 5 ingredients and cook slowly, covered for 1 hr. Add applesauce, carrots and onion; cook 1 more hr. Add apple and cook till tender.

Apple-Pecan-Cornbread Dressing

1 pan cornbread, crumbled
1 8oz. pkg. stuffing mix
2 T. parsley, chopped
1/2 t. salt
1/2 t. ground ginger
3/4 c. butter

1 c. celery, sliced
1 c. onion, chopped
2 c. apple cider
2 c. apples, chopped
3 eggs, beaten
1/2 c. chopped pecans

Melt butter in lg. pan; sauté celery and onion. Add all other ingredients mixing well. Lightly stuff into body and neck cavity of turkey 16 to 18 lbs.

Apple Sausage Breakfast Ring

2 lbs. lean bulk pork
   sausage
2 lg. eggs, slightly beaten
1-1/2 c. crushed Ritz
   crackers

1 c. grated apple, peeled
1/2 c. minced onion
1/4 c. milk

Line 2-1/2 qt. ring mold with plastic wrap or waxed paper. Combine all ingredients, mix well and press firmly into mold and chill several hrs. or overnight. Unmold, removing plastic paper onto a baking sheet with raised edges.

Bake at 350F for 1 hr. Transfer onto a serving platter; fill center of ring with scrambled eggs. Yield 8 servings.

What is more melancholy than the old apple-trees that linger about the spot where once stood a homestead, but where there is now only a ruined chimney rising out of a grassy and weed-grown cellar? They offer their fruit to every wayfarer--apples that are bitter-sweet with the moral of time's vicissitude.

Apple, Pork Chop Casserole

4 center cut pork chops   1 t. cinnamon
4 lg. cooking apples   2 T. butter
2 T. brown sugar

Trim fat from chops and brown quickly in skillet over high heat. Peel core and slice the apples. Place in lightly greased casserole. Sprinkle brown sugar and cinnamon over the apples. Dot with butter. Place browned pork chops on top. Cover and bake in 400F oven for 45 min.

Apple Orchard Bean Bake

1 lb. bulk pork sausage   1/4 t. pepper
1 lb. 4 oz. pork & beans in   1 lg. unpared apple, cored,
   molasses sauce   and thinly sliced
1/2 can tomato soup   1/4 c. brown sugar, packed
   (10-1/2 oz.)

Heat oven to 450F. (I use a 375F-400F oven) Brown sausage in skillet. Drain off excess fat. Stir in beans, soup and pepper. Pour into 1-1/2 qt. casserole. Arrange apple slices over top; sprinkle with brown sugar. Bake uncovered 25 min. or until apples are tender. Remove from oven. Let stand 5-10 min., until beans absorb juices. Serves 6.

Apples, Yammy

4 med. baking apples	1 T. butter or margarine,
1 8 oz. can sweet potatoes,	melted
drained and mashed	1/2 t. cinnamon
3 T. brown sugar	1/4 t. salt
3 T. maple syrup	3 T. slivered almonds

Wash and core apples; remove enough pulp to make the opening about 2" wide. Chop the pulp and mix with remaining ingredients, setting aside 1 T. almonds. Wrap a 7" square of aluminum foil around bottom and sides of apple. Fill apple cavities with sweet potato mixture; sprinkle with almonds. Bake uncovered for 1 hr. or until tender.

Good accompanied to any main meat dish. But especially so with ham and poultry. 350F oven, use 1/4 -1/2 c. water in bottom of baking dish.

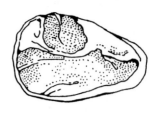

Apples, Spiced Pork Roast

3-4 lb. pork roast
1/2 t. salt
1/4 t. pepper
1/2 t. ginger
1/2 t. cinnamon
1 T. onion powder

1/4 c. brown sugar
1/4 c. flour
2 T. margarine or oil
1/2 c. apple juice
2 sweet apples, peeled and
    quartered

Mix flour, sugar and seasonings; rub onto surface of roast. Brown roast in margarine or oil. Insert a meat thermometer into thickest part of roast. Put roast and apple juice into a roasting pan. Cook in a 325F oven for 1-1/2 hrs. or until thermometer reaches 140F; add water to pan if necessary during roasting period. Add apples, turning to coat in pan juices. Continue cooking until thermometer reaches 170F.

PIES

Apple, Rhubarb & Pineapple Pie

Crust:

2 c. all-purpose flour

1 t. salt

1/2 t. baking powder

2/3 c. Crisco shortening

4 to 5 T. ice water

Filling:

1 c. sugar

3 T. all-purpose flour

1 t. salt

1 c. peeled, chopped
McIntosh apples

1 t. lemon juice

2 c. fresh or frozen
unsweetened rhubard

1/2 c. drained canned
crushed pineapple

1/4 c. honey

1 T. butter or margarine

To make crust: In med. mixing bowl, combine flour, salt and baking powder (if used). Using pastry blender or 2 knives, cut in shortening until all flour is blended in to form pea-size chunks. Sprinkle with water, 1 T. at a time. Using fork, toss lightly until dough will form a ball. Press between hands for form two 5- to 6- inch "pancakes." Wrap in plastic wrap. Refrigerate while preparing filling.

To make filling: In small mixing bowl, combine sugar, flour and salt. Place apple slices in large bowl. Sprinkle with lemon juice. Add rhubarb, pineapple and sugar mixture. Toss to mix.

To roll crust: Lightly flour rolling surface and rolling pin. Roll dough for bottom crust into circle. Trim 1" larger than up-side-down 9-1/2" deep-dish pie plate. Loosen dough carefully. Fold into quarters. Unfold and press into pie plate. Leave overhang on crust. Roll top crust same as bottom. Cut into 10-1/2" wide strips.

To bake pie: Spoon filling into unbaked pie shell. Drizzle with honey. Dot with butter. Moisten pastry overhang with water. Make lattice top over filling. Trim ends of strips even with crust overhang. Press edges together. Fold overhang up and onto rim of pie plate. Press and flute. Place pie in 450F oven. Immediately reduce heat to 350F. Bake for 60 to 75 min., or until filling in center is bubbly and crust is golden brown. Cool to room temp. before serving.

Pie

No Cholesterol Pie Crust

2-1/4 c. unbleached flour
1 t. salt

2/3 c. sunflower oil
1/3 c. skim milk

Mix flour and salt; add milk to oil and whip with a fork. Add to flour mixture and mix gently. Makes top and bottom crusts. Roll out as usual.

Apple Crunch Pie

Crust:

Unbaked 9" single pie crust made with all-vegetable shortening adding 2 T. finely crushed granola to flour.

Filling and Topping:

2-1/2 to 3 c. cored, pared and tinly sliced apples (about 1 lb. or 3 med. apples)
1/2 c. all-vegetable butter flavor shortening or margarine, divided
2 eggs

1 can (14 oz.) sweetened condensed milk (NOT evaporated milk)
1 t. maple flavor
1/2 t. cinnamon
1/8 t. nutmeg
1/2 c. firm pkd. brown sugar
1/2 c. all-purpose flour
1/4 c. finely crushed granola

Heat oven to 425F.
Filling: Arrange apples in unbaked pie shell. Melt 1/4 c. shortening. Beat eggs in med. bowl. Add sweetened condensed milk, melted shortening, maple flavor, cinnamon and nutmeg. Mix well. Pour over apples.
Topping: Combine sugar and flour in med. bowl. Cut in remaining 1/4 c. shortening until crumbly. Stir in granola. Sprinkle over custard. Bake at 425F for 10 min. Reduce oven temp. to 375F. Bake at 375F for 35 to 40 min. or until golden brown. (Cover top or edge of pie with foil, if necessary, to prevent overbrowning.) Serve warm, at room temp. or chilled. One 9" pie.

APPLE-PIE BED

The apple-pie bed is a practical joke that still survives after more than a century of practice. A joker secretly makes another's bed with the sheets folded in a special way. Then the joker and his accomplices watch the victim get into bed and struggle to lie down, the folded sheets preventing him from getting his legs down.

The apple-pie bed has always been popular in school and prison dormitories, where practical jokers have easy access to the beds of others. It has also been worked on the "first night" beds of newlyweds.

Apple Pie, Dutch

1 qt. peeled, sliced, tart
   apples
3 T. melted butter

3/4 c. sugar
1/4 t. cinnamon
1/4 t. nutmeg

Topping:
3/4 c. flour
1/2 t. cinnamon

1/3 c. brown sugar
1/3 c. butter

Blend sliced apples with melted butter so each slice is coated. Add sugar and spices; mix. Make streusel topping by combining flour, cinnamon and brown sugar. Cream butter until soft and work dry ingredients into it until crumbly. Pour apples into an unbaked pie shell, cover with streusel topping. Bake at 450F for 20 min., then 350F for 40 min.

Note: This is our favorite apple pie. I have used this recipe for over 40 years.

Apple Pie

1/2 c. sour cream	1/2 t. cinnamon
2 T. flour	1/4 t. nutmeg
3/4 c. sugar	dash of salt

Sprinkle Topping:

1/2 c. flour	1/4 t. cinnamon
1/2 c. brown sugar	1/3 c. butter

Peel and slice 6 to 8 apples. Combine 1/2 c. sour cream with 2 T. flour, 3/4 c. sugar, 1/2 t. cinnamon, 1/4 t. nutmeg and a dash of salt. Toss this with the apples, fill pastry shell. Sprinkle the following over the top of the pie: 1/2 c. flour 1/2 c. brown sugar, 1/4 t. cinnamon, and 1/3 c. butter; mixed well together. Bake at 400F for 50 min.

Apple Pie, Crunchy

2 c. Cortland apples, chopped	1/2 t. vanilla extract
1/2 c. pkd. brown sugar	1/2 t. freshly squeezed lemon juice
1/2 c. granulated sugar	1/2 c. pecans, chopped
1/2 c. all-purpose flour	1 9" unbaked pie shell
1 egg	

Put chopped apples in a lg. bowl. Separate egg yolk and egg white into two sm. mixing bowls (save egg white for another use.) Beat egg yolk and mix well with brown and granulated sugar, flour, vanilla, lemon juice and pecans; add to chopped apples. Stir well and pour mixture into unbaked pie shell. Bake at 350F for 30-45 min., or until apples are tender and brown.

Apple Pie, French

Pastry for single pie crust
3 c. Haralson apples
1 t. cinnamon
3/4 c. sugar
pinch of salt

Topping:
1/2 c. butter
1 c. flour
1/2 c. brown sugar

Put filling mixture in pie shell. Mix topping ingredients until crumbly. Sprinkle over top of apples. Bake at 350F for 50 min.

Apple Custard Pie

Pastry for 2 crust pie:
1/2 c. sugar
2 eggs
3 lg. tart apples, peeled, cored and sliced

1 c. milk
1/2 t. nutmeg
1/2 t. cinnamon

Prepare pastry and lined 9" pie plate. Cook the apples in a heavy saucepan with a sm. amount of water; add sugar and spices. Separate eggs. Beat egg yolks and add to the milk, then stir into cooked apples. Beat egg whites until stiff. Fold into apple mixture. Pour into pie shell and cover with top pastry. Bake at 350F for 30 min., until center of pie is firm.

Apple Pie, Extra Elegant

2 T. flour
1/2 t. salt
3/4 c. sugar
1 egg

1 c. sour cream
1/2 t. vanilla
2 c. apples, chopped

Sift together, flour, salt and sugar. Add eggs, sour cream and vanilla; beat well. Stir in finely chopped apples. If apples are not tart, add 1 T. of lemon juice. Place this mixture in a 9" shell. Bake 15 min at 425F, then 30 min. at 350F. Sprinkle with topping.

Topping:
1/3 c. sugar
1/3 c. flour
dash of salt

1 t. cinnamon
1/4 c. butter

Cut dry ingredients into butter. Sprinkle mixture over pie and bake for 10 min. at 400F.

But I, When I undress me
Each night, upon my knees
Will ask the Lord to bless me
With apple pie and cheese!

Apple Raisin Cream Pie

7-8 c. tart apple slices	3/4 c. raisins
1 c. sugar	1/8 t. salt
1/2 c. flour	1-2 t. grated lemon rind
1/2 t. nutmeg	4 t. butter
1 t. cinnamon	3/4 c. heavy cream

Make pastry for a 2 crust pie. Line bottom of a 10" pie pan with 1 crust. Combine apple slices, sugar, flour, spices, raisins, salt and lemon peel; mix together well. Spoon filling into pastry-lined pan; dot with butter. Cover with top crust; seal edges. Be sure to cut in steam vents. Cut a 1" circle in center of top crust. Bake at 400F for 40-45 min. Remove pie from oven; slowly pour cream into center hole of top crust. Return to oven; bake 5-10 min. longer. Let stand 5 min. before cutting. Because this contains a milk product, be sure to refrigerate leftovers.

Apple Pie, Caramel

24 caramels	2 T. sugar
1 T. milk	1/2 c. applesauce
1 graham crumb pie crust	2 t. vanilla
1/3 c. chopped nuts	1/2 t. cinnamon
1 8-oz. pkg. cream cheese, softened	8-oz. whipped topping
1/2 c. sour cream	fresh apple slices

Melt caramels with milk over low heat, or in microwave at high for 1 to 1-1/2 min., stirring until smooth. Pour into crust; sprinkle with nuts. Cool. Beat cream cheese, sour cream and sugar until smooth. Stir in applesauce, vanilla and cinnamon. Fold in 1/2 of the whipped topping. Spread over caramel in crust. Chill at least 4 hrs. Garnish with remaining whipped topping and apple slices. Store any leftover pie in refrigerator.

Apple-Blackberry Pie

Pastry for double-crust 9"pie:

3 c. fresh blackberries	3 T. quick cooking tapioca
1 c. peeled and thinly sliced apples	1/2 t. ground cinnamon
1 c. sugar	2 T. butter OR margarine

Roll 1/2 of pastry to 1/8" thickness, and fit into a 9" pieplate. Combine blackberries and apple slices; place in pastry shell. Combine sugar, tapioca, and cinnamon; stir well. Sprinkle sugar mixture over blackberries; dot with butter. Roll out remaining pastry to 1/8" thickness, and place over filling. Trim pastry; seal and flute edges. Cut slits in top for steam to escape. Bake at 350 for 1 hr. or until golden brown. Cool before serving. Yield: 1 9" pie.

I have upset my apple-cart; I am done for.
I've upset the apple-cart!
The apple-Cart.

Apple Pie, Grandmother's

6-1/2 c. peeled and thinly
  sliced apples
  (about 5 apples)
1 c. water
3/4 c. sugar

1/4 to 1/2 t. ground allspice
pinch of salt
pastry for double-crust 9"
  pie

Combine apples and water in a lg. saucepan; bring to a boil.
Cover, reduce heat, and simmer 10 min. or until apples are
tender. Drain well. Return to saucepan. Mash slightly with a
potato masher. Stir in sugar, allspice, and salt, mixing well.

Roll 1/2 of pastry to 1/8" thickness, and fit into a 9" pieplate.
Spoon apple mixture into pieplate. Roll remaining pastry to
1/8" thickness. Cover pie with crust. Trim pastry; seal and
flute edges. Cut slits to make an apple design in top crust
for steam to escape. Use extra pastry to make a leafshaped
cutout; add cutout to apple design. Bake at 375F for 45
min., or until golden brown. Cover edges with foil to prevent
overbrowning. Yield: 1 9" pie.

Apple-Honey Custard Pie

1 9" unbaked pie shell	1 c. yogurt
2 c. peeled, sliced apples	1 t. vanilla
4 lg. eggs	1/2 t. cinnamon
3/4 c. honey	1/4 t. salt
	1/4 c. walnuts (Opt)

Spread apple slices evenly over pie shell. Combine remaining ingredients in the blender and run at high speed for several seconds. Pour custard mixture over apples. Sprinkle on some walnuts if desired. Bake at 375F for 45 min. or until solid when a cold knife is inserted. Cool at least to room temperature before cutting. Store leftovers in refrigerator.

Apple Pie, Old Fashioned

any 2 crust pie recipe	1 T. flour
6 c. sliced pie apples	cinnamon
1 c. white sugar	butter

Roll out bottom crust. Add apples with sugar, flour and cinnamon. Dot with butter. Put top crust on and sprinkle with sugar. Bake at 375F for 30-35 min.

Apple Pie, Norweigan

1 egg
3/4 c. sugar
1 t. vanilla
1 t. baking powder
1/4 t. salt

1/2 c. flour
1/2 c. chopped black
   walnuts
1 c. fresh diced apples

Combine all ingredients in a lg. mixing bowl; stir until well-blended. Turn mixture into a buttered 8" pie plate. Mixture will be stiff. Bake for 30 min at 350F or until golden brown. Serve warm or cool. Cut into wedges and serve with Cool Whip.

SALADS

Apple-Chicken Party Salad

3 c. cold cooked chicken cut into lg. chunks	salt and pepper
	1/2 c. mayonnaise
1 lg. red eating apple, cored and diced	1 c. green grapes
	1/2 c. salted almonds
1 T. lemon juice	

Toss chicken and apple in lg. bowl. Stir together juice, seasoning and mayonnaise. Fold with grapes into chicken. Chill for several hours. Pile into serving bowl lined with ruffly lettuce or serve individually into lettuce cups. Garnish with almonds. Serves 6.

Curry Dressing:

2/3 c. vegetable oil	1/2 t. onion powder
1/2 c. white wine vinegar	1/8 t. white pepper
1 T. chopped chutney	dash of cayenne pepper
1/2 t. curry powder	

Turn lettuce into a chilled salad bowl. Cut apples in 1/2 and core; slice thinly. Arrange apples and crab over the lettuce. Toss with curry dressing. Serve with assorted condiments. Makes about 6 servings.

To prepare dressing; combine oil vinegar, chutney, curry powder, onion powder, white pepper and cayenne; mix well. Let stand 1 hr. or longer to blend flavors. Mix well before serving. Makes about 1-1/3 c.

Snicker Salad

1 8 oz. cont. Cool Whip   2 Snicker candy bar
2 apples   2 bananas

Put Cool Whip in bowl, dice the apples with peeling on into Cool Whip. Cut up the Snickers and slice the bananas. Fold all into Cool Whip.

The woman whom thou gavest to be with me,
she gave me of the tree,
and I did eat.

Apple Salad, Turkey

1 5 oz. can turkey or fresh   2 T. raisins
    baked turkey chunks   1 T. brown sugar
3/4 c. chopped apples   1/2 c. Italian dressing
1/2 c. sliced celery

In med. bowl gently stir together all ingredients except brown sugar and dressing. Stir together sugar and dressing and pour over turkey mixture. Toss gently and serve on lettuce.

Apple Salad, Indian Style

1 qt. shredded head lettuce
3 Cortland apples (med.)
1 (8 oz.) pkg. imitation crab or reg. crab (canned or frozen)
Condiments such as salted peanuts, toasted sesame seeds or sunflower seeds, raisins, chutney or chopped hard cooked eggs.

Apple Cheddar Salad

2 apples, quartered and   6 oz. cheddar cheese cut
   thinly sliced   into small cubes
2 t. lemon juice   1/4 c. mayonnaise
2 c. celery, thinly sliced

Place apples in sm. bowl; toss with lemon juice. Add celery and other ingredients; toss to coat. Serve on lettuce - lined plate.
209 calories per serving
4 servings

Apple and Tuna Salad

1 (7 oz.) can tuna
2 apples (Cortland)
1-1/2 c. chopped celery
2-1/2 T. mayonnaise

2 T. lemon juice
1/2 t. salt
dash of pepper

Flake tuna. Core and cut 2 Cortland apples in 1/2" cuts to make 1 c.; add to tuna. Then add celery, mayonnaise (thinned with lemon juice) salt and pepper. Mix lightly with a fork. Serve on lettuce.

Apple Salad, Cinnamon

1/2 c. red cinnamon candies
1/2 c. sugar

2 c. water
6 apples, peeled and cored

Filling:
3 pitted dates, chopped
1/3 c. drained crushed pineapple

2 T. broken nuts
2-3 T. mayonnaise

Cook candies and sugar in water until dissolved. Add apples and cook until tender. Chill. Combine filling ingredients. Stuff into core hole of apples. Serve on lettuce leaf garnished with an apple leaf. Use a bit of cinnamon stick for stem. Makes 6 servings.

Apple-Turkey Salad

1 can Swanson chunk white (or white & dark) turkey, drained (5 oz.)
3/4 c. chopped apple

1/2 c. sliced celery
2 T. raisins
1/3 c. prepared Italian dressing
1 T. brown sugar

In med. bowl, gently stir together turkey, apple, celery, and raisins. In a cup stir together dressing and brown sugar; pour over turkey mixture. Toss gently to coat. Serve on lettuce leaves. Makes 1-1/2 c. or 2 servings.

Apple Salad-Kids-Make, Terrific

1. Cut up 1/4 apple.
2. Chop 2 walnuts.
3. Cut up 1 celery stick.
4. Mix in bowl.
5. Add 6 raisins.
6. Stir in 1 T. of mayonnaise.
7. Eat.

Apple-Cherry Salad

1 c. boiling water
1 pkg. (3 oz.) cherry flavored
   gelatin
1 c. cranberry juice
1 T. lemon juice

2 tart apples, chopped
   (about 2-1/2 c.)
1/2 c. thinly sliced celery
1/3 c. chopped nuts (opt)

Pour boiling water on gelatin; stir until gelatin is dissolved. Stir in cranberry juice and lemon juice. Refrigerate unitl slightly thickened. Stir in remaining ingredients. Pour into 4 c. mold. Refrigerate until firm; unmold.

Like the sweet apple which reddens upon the
topmost bough

A-top on the topmost twig--which the pluckers
forgot, somehow--

Forgot it not, nay, but got it not, for none
could get it till now.

Apple-Carrot Salad

Peel and grate 4 c. apples and 4 c. carrots. Stir in 1 c. raisins and add 1/2 c. mayonnaise or yogurt. Mix and chill.

Apple Coleslaw

4 c. shredded green	1 T. vinegar
cabbage	1 t. salt
1-1/2 c. diced unpared	1/4 t. pepper
apple	1/2 t. sugar
1/4 c. chopped walnuts	1 T. milk
1/2 c. raisins	1/2 c. mayonnaise

Toss cabbage with apples, nuts and raisins. Refrigerate. In
a sm. bowl, combine rest of the ingredients and refrigerate.
To serve: pour dressing on cabbage mixture and toss.

Apple Salad, Taffy

1 lg. can chunk pineapple in
   unsweetened natural juice
   drain and save juice
1/2 c. sugar
1 egg
1-1/2 T. vinegar
1 T. flour
1 c. peanuts
2 c. minature marshmellows
1 lg. Cool Whip
2-3 diced apples, unpeeled

Night before: in saucepan, mix pineapple juice, sugar, well-beaten egg, vinegar and flour. Mix on med. heat until thick, stirring constantly. Refrigerate overnite. Next day: Mix sauce and Cool Whip. Fold in other ingredients. Chill.

Apple Salad, Fresh

Diabetic, low in salt, sugar and fat.

8 c. chopped, tart red
   apples, unpeeled
1 can (20 oz.) pineapple
   chunks, drained
   (reserve juice)

2 c. seedless green grapes
1-2 t. poppy seeds
1-1/2 c. toasted pecans

Dressing:
reserved pineapple juice
1/4 c. butter
1/4 c. sugar
1 T. lemon juice
2 T. cornstarch

2 T. water
1 c. mayonnaise or 1/2 c.
   reduced calorie mayon-
   naise and 1/2 c. plain
   yogurt

Make dressing first by combining the reserved pineapple juice, butter, sugar and lemon juice in a sm. saucepan. Heat to boiling. Combine the cornstarch and water to make a smooth paste; add to the hot mixture; cook until thick and smooth. Chill completely before stirring in mayonnaise/yogurt. Combine apples, pineapple chunks, grapes and poppy seeds in lg. glass bowl. Add chilled dressing, refrigerate until time to serve. Stir in pecans right before serving for maximum cruchiness. Yield: 16 servings. Diabetic changes: one serving equals 1-1/2 fruits, 3 fats; also 206 calories, 86 mg sodium, 12 mg cholesterol, 22 gm carbohydrate, 2 gm protein, 14 gm fat.

Gold Marinate Mushroom Salad

1/2 lb. mushrooms, sliced
1 Golden Delicious apple,
   cored and sliced

4 c. cut/torn Romaine lettuce
1-2 oz. blue cheese, crumbled
crisp bacon bits, opt.

Marinade:
1/4 c. vegetable oil
3 T. lemon juice
1 t. Dijon mustard
1 clove garlic, crushed

1/2- t. crushed oregano
1/2 t. sugar
1/4 t. salt
1/8 t. freshly ground pepper

Combine mushrooms, apple and marinade. Marinate at least 30 min. Remove garlic. Combine mushroom mixture, lettuce and cheese. Sprinkle with bacon if desired. Makes 4-6 servings.

To prepare marinade: Combine oil, lemon juice, mustard, garlic, oregano, sugar, salt and pepper. Make about 1/2 c.

Applesauce Salad, Cinnamon

1 T. red cinnamon candy	1/2 c. chopped walnuts
1 c. hot water	2 c. sweetened applesauce
1 pkg. cherry Jell-O	1/2 c. chopped celery

Melt cinnamon candy in hot water and if necesary, heat until dissolved. Pour over gelatin stirring to dissolve. Add applesauce and chill until partially set. Fold in celery and nuts; chill until firm.

Apple Salad, Christmas Broccoli

1 lb. fresh broccoli flowerets and chopped stems	1 apple, chopped
1/2 c. raisins	1/2 c. chopped walnuts or pecans
1 lg. red onion, chopped	1/2 lb. bacon, cooked and crumbled

Mix first 6 ingredients together. Mix your favorite dressing and pour over other ingredients.

Apple Surprise

6 slices bacon, diced
1/3 c. slivered almonds
1 head lettuce
3 green onions, sliced
2 Cortland apples, diced
1/4 c. oil

3 T. tarregon vinegar
1 t. sugar
1/2 t. dry mustard
1/8 t. salt
dash pepper

Cook diced bacon until crisp; drain and reserve 1 T. drippings. Lightly brown almonds in drippings. Mix oil, vinegar,
sugar, mustard, salt and pepper. Tear bite-size pieces of
lettuce into salad bowl; add remaining ingredients and toss
with dressing. (To prepare ahead, combine ingredients
except apples and dressing and refrigerate.)

THE ADAPTABLE APPLE

Apple Dip, Taffy

8-oz. cream cheese
1/2 c. brown sugar
1 t. vanilla

1/2 t. carmel flavor OR
    maple syrup
chopped nuts

Cream cheese and add the rest of ingredients.

Art thou the topmost apple
The gatherers could reach,
Reddening on the bough?
Shall I not take thee?

Apple Pie Filling

4-1/2 c. sugar
1 c. cornstarch
2 t. ground cinnamon
1/4 t. nutmeg
3 T. lemon juice

2-3 drops yellow food color
5-1/2 to 6 lbs. tart apples
   (any good pie apple, OK)
10 c. water

Take first 4 ingredients and mix in at least a 6 qt. pan. Add salt and 10 c. water. Mix well and cook until thick and bubbly, stirring often. Remove from heat, add lemon juice and food coloring. Pack sliced apples into hot clean jars, leaving 1"-2" headspace. Fill with hot syrup. Gently remove air spaces with knife. Put on hot lids and process in water bath 20 min. 2 qt. make 1 9" pie.

Apples, Debbie's Dip

8-oz. softened cream
   cheese
1/4 c. brown sugar

1/4 c. white sugar
1 t. vanilla
1/2 c. chopped salted
   peanuts

Beat together cream cheese, sugars and vanilla. Stir in peanuts. Use as a dip for fresh apple slices.

Apples

Wash, pare, and core. Cut into desired size, if peeled fruit is to stand several min. before pre-cooking drop into mild salt solution to prevent discoloration and drain. Boil 3-5 min. in a med. syrup. Pack into jars within 1/2" of top. Fill with boiling syrup. Put on cap screw band firmly tight.
Process pints: 20 min.   ]
    quarts: 25 min.   ] in boiling water bath.
Syrup is 1 c. of sugar to 2 c. of water.

Apple Jelly

2 T. unflavored gelatin
1 qt. unsweetened apple
   juice

2 T. lemon juice, strained
2 T. artificial liquid
   sweetender

In kettle soften gelatin in apple juice and add lemon juice.
Bring to a boil dissolving gelatin, boil 1 min. Remove from
heat. Stir in liquid sweetener. Pour into sterilized jelly glasses 1/2" from top. Cover with parafin or put on cap,
screwband tight. When cool store in refrigerator.
Yields: 4 half pints.

Apple Butter

16 c. applesauce
8 c. sugar
1 t. cloves

1 T. cinnamon
1/2 t. allspice

Simmer in 325F oven 2 hrs. or until thick. Pour into hot jars
and seal at once.

Apples are known as the "King of Fruits."

Applesauce-IceCream, Half Bake

6 Haralson apples   1 t. cinnamon
1/2 c. sugar

Peel, core and thinly slice apples. Mix in lg. microwave bowl with sugar and cinnamon to taste. Microwave for 10 min., stir and microwave 10 min. more. Apples will still be slightly crisp. Cook longer if desired. Serve hot over ice cream.

Apple Jam
Yield: 5 qt.

6 lb. cooking apples	1/3 c. ground ginger (opt)
5 c. water	14 c. sugar
rind and juice of 4 lemons	

Peel, core and chop the apples. Tie the peel and core in cheesecloth and put with the apples and water into a preserving pan. Add the finely grated lemon rind and the juice, together with the ginger, if used. Cook until pulpy, then squeeze out and discard the cheesecloth bag. Stir in the sugar and boil until set.

Apple Dip, Fall

1 pkg. cream cheese, room temperature (8-oz.)	1 c. salted chopped peanuts red and green crisp apples
3/4 c. brown sugar	orange juice
1 t. vanilla	

Blend together all ingredients except last two. Wash and slice apples; dip in orange juice. Drain. Arrange in circle on pretty plate and place the dip in center in a bowl. Sprinkle additional chopped peanuts of top of dip. Refrigerate leftovers.

Apple Butter, Slo-Cooker

12-14 cooking apples   2 c. sugar
   (16 c. chopped)   1 t. ground cinnamon
2 c. cider   1/4 t. ground cloves

Core and chop apples, do not peel. Combine apples and cider in slow cooking pot. Cover and cook on low for 10-12 hrs. or until apples are mushy. Stir occassionally. Puree in food mill or sieve. Return pureed mixture to pot; add sugar and spices. Cover and cook on low 1-2 hrs. until hot and until spices have blended in. Makes about 8 c.
Can be kept several ways:
1. Will keep several weeks in refrigerator.
2. Pour into hot, sterilized jars and seal. (water bath 20 min.)
3. Pour into freezer container and freeze.

Apple Butter

16 c. thick apple pulp   8 c. sugar
1 c. vinegar (Opt.)   4 t. cinnamon

Core and slice apples, **do not peel.** Add only enough water to cook apples until soft. Press through fine sieve and measure. Combine all ingredients. Cook until mixture remains in a smooth mass when a little cooled (about 1-1/2 hrs. boiling. During cooking stir frequently to prevent burning, pour into sterilized jars to 1/2" from top. Put on cap, screw band firmly tight, process in boiling water bath 10 min. or put in pressure cooker 5 min. with 10 lb. pressure.

Apples, Stuffed

Apples   OR   Apples
cream cheese   cheese spread
chopped nuts   chopped celery

Wash and core apples. Mix cream cheese and nuts or cheese spread and celery. Stuff cavity of apple with chosen filling. Cover and chill for 1 hr. before serving.

It takes about forty leaves to make enough food
for one apple to grow to its full size.

Apple Butter

8 qt. sweet apple cider
6 qts. or(8 lbs.) pared and
   quartered apples (I use
   1/2 McIntosh,
   1/2 Wealthy)

4 c. sugar
2 t. ground cinnamon
2 t. ground ginger
1 t. cloves

Heat cider to boiling in lg. Dutch oven. Boil uncovered until cider measures 4 qts. about 1-1/4 hrs. Add apples. Heat to boiling; reduce heat. Simmer uncovered, stirring frequently, until apples are soft and can be broken apart with spoon, about 1 hr. (Apples can be pressed through sieve or food mill at this point if smooth apple butter is desired.)

Stir in remaining ingredients. Heat to boiling; reduce heat. Simmer uncovered, stirring frequently, until no liquid separates from pulp, about 2 hrs. Heat to boiling. Immediately pour mixture into hot jars, leaving 1/4" headspace. Wipe rim of jars. Seal and process in boiling water bath 10 min. Makes about 6 half-pts. butter.

Apple Pie in a Jar

7 qts. peeled, sliced cooking apples (about 7 lbs.)

Syrup:

4-1/2 c. sugar	1 t. salt
1 c. cornstarch	10 c. water
2 t. cinnamon	3 T. lemon juice
1/4 t. nutmeg	

Peel and slice apples; fill hot jars with apples, leaving 1" headspace. Make syrup by combining sugar, cornstarch, cinnamon, nutmeg, salt and water; cook until thick. Add lemon juice. Pour syrup over apples in jars, leaving 1/2" headspace. Adjust lids. Process 20 min. in boiling water bath. Yield: 7 qt.

Crafts

1. For an attractive, natural table centerpiece for fall, arrange Golden Delicious, Honey Gold or NorthWestern Greening apples in a bowl with bright colored leaves.

2. For the Christmas holidays, select the reddest apples available, then wash and polish them until they shine. Pile on a wooden tray with sprigs of evergreen.

3. For attractive Christmas candle holders, choose two large red apples that sit up straight. Carve out the stem end just enough to fit candle in (whatever size you want.) A green candle really looks nice.

Apple Candlesticks

Wash and polish a large Connell Red apple. Remove core from the stem end about 2/3 of the way down into the apple. Insert candle. Use individually or arrange several as a table centerpiece.

Apple Butter

2 lbs. apples, cored, peeled   2 c. brown sugar
   and quartered   1 t. cinnamon
1 c. apple cider   1/4 t. ground cloves

Place apples in heavy saucepan with cider. Cook covered over low heat until tender. Blend pulp with a wire whisk. Stir in sugar and spices. Cook, stirring until thick. Serve on warm toast or fresh bread.

> The fruit
> Of that forbidden tree, whose mortal taste
> Brought death into the world, and all our woe.

Apple Snacks

1. For a favorite fall snack, make apple shish kebabs by combining cut-up apples with marshmallows and bananas.

2. Spread crunchy peanut butter on apple wedges for a quick and healthy snack.

3. When making caramel apples roll dipped apple end in chopped peanuts and mini chocolate chip mixture for a special treat.

4. Top a toasted English muffin with applesauce and grated sharp cheese or cinnamon.

5. For Apple-Mint Tea, combine 4 c. sweet apple cider or apple juice with 1-1/2 c. of chopped fresh spearmint. Microwave or cook on stove top until mixture boils. Let steep 30 min; strain.

6. Try this simple way to make dried apples. Peel, core and half 2 qts. apples. Shread the apples coarsely onto buttered cookie sheet; bake at 225F until dry. Remove from cookie sheet with pancake turner. Break in pieces; store in airtight container.

Apple Cartwheels

8 apples   1/2 c. peanut butter
6-oz. chocolate chips   1 T. honey
1/4 c. raisins

Remove cores from apples, leaving a 1-1/4" diameter cavity.
Process chocolate chips in a blender 5 sec. until chopped.
In a sm. bowl mix chips, raisins, peanut butter and honey.
Stuff cored apples with this mixture. Wrap apples in plastic
wrap and chill. Slice crosswise into 1/2" slices to serve.
Makes about 32 slices.

Apple Jelly, Herbed

2-1/2 c. apple cider	3 c. sugar
2 4" sprigs fresh herbs,	1 pouch liquid pectin
basil, rosemary or thyme	

Prepare home canning jars and lids according to manfactur-
er's instructions. Jars should be covered with water and
boiled 10-15 min. to sterilize. Reserve 3 or 4 herb leaves; set
aside. Place remaining sprigs of herbs in cheesecloth bag.
Simmer apple cider and herbs in cheesecloth bag in a
covered saucepan for 10 min. Stir in sugar. Increase heat;
bring to a full rolling boil. Boil hard 1 min. and remove from
heat; discard bag of herbs. Stir in pectin. Carefully ladle into
hot, sterilized jars, leaving 1/8" headspace. Place a reserved
herb leaf in each jar. Adjust caps. Invert for a few sec., then
stand upright to cool. Yield: about 3 8-oz. jars.

Apple Snacks

1. For a favorite fall snack, make apple shisk kebabs by
combining cut-up apples with marshmallows, bananas
and/or grapes.

2. Spread crunchy peanut butter on apple wedges for a
quick healthy snack.

3. Make "mini" carameled apples by dipping quartered
apples on tooth picks or fondue forks into melted caramel.

> The apple blossoms' shower of pearl,
> Though blent with rosier hue,
> As beautiful as woman's blush, --
> As evanescent too.

Apples, Pie

1 gal. apples peeled and sliced
1 c. sugar

Peel and slice apples, add 1 c. sugar. Let stand covered for 12 hrs. Fill jars with apples; seal and process 20 min. in hot water. Excellent for pie.

Apples, Mock Caramel Dip for

8-oz. pkg. cream cheese,   1/2 c. brown sugar
   softened   2 t. vanilla

Beat with mixer until smooth. Serve with sliced apples for dipping.

Apples, Cheese Dip for

8-oz. pkg. cream cheese,   1 c. grated cheddar cheese
   softened   1 T. Blue cheese crumbled,
1 jar Kraft Olde English   (optional)
   cheese spread

Mix until smooth. If too stiff, add a little milk. Spread on sliced apples.

Apple Rings, Cinnamon

18 tart apples
6 c. sugar
3 c. water

1 9-oz. pkg. red cinnamon
   candies
3 drops red food color

Cut cored, peeled apples in rings. Combine sugar, water, cinnamon candies and food color, bring to a boil; boil 3 min. Add apples to syrup, cook until transparent. Pack in hot jars, cover with syrup. Adjust lids. Process in boiling water bath 25 min. Makes 4 pt.

It is more pleasant to pluck an apple from the branch
than to take one from a graven dish.

The apples she had gathered smelt most sweet.

Apples, Fried

2 qt. small tart apples,	1 t. cinnamon
unpeeled	3 T. butter
1 c. light brown sugar	

Cut each apple into 6 wedges; core. Place in 10" skillet. Sprinkle with brown sugar and cinnamon; dot with butter. Cover with lid or foil.

Place skillet on cold burner; turn heat to low. Cook, stirring only occasionally, until tender, about 45 min. Uncover and cook 3 to 5 min. longer. Serve warm. Makes 8 servings.

Apple Salsa

Mix together:
1-1/2 c. diced cherry tomatoes
3/4 c. diced, unpeeled tart green apples
3/4 c. diced, yellow sweet pepper
3 green onions, sliced
3 T. lemon juice
1-1/2 T. vegeatble oil
1-1/2 T. drained capers, chopped (optional)
2-1/4 t. dried rosemary leaves, crushed
1/2 t. sugar
1/2 t. salt
1/8 t. pepper

Cover and refrigerate 2 hours. Makes 2-3/4 cup.

Apple pies and apple fritters,
apple cores to feed the critters.
Johnny Appleseed 1774-1855

Need a Gift?

For

• Shower • Birthday • Mother's Day •
• Anniversary • Christmas •

Turn Page For Order Form

TO ORDER COPIES OF

the
Adaptable Apple

Please send me _____ copies of the Adaptable Apple at $9.95 each. (Make checks payable to Hearts 'N Tummies.)
Add $3.00 S/H

Name _____

Street _____

City_____ State_____ Zip Code _____

Hearts 'N Tummies Cookbook Co.
3544 Blakslee Street
Wever, IA 52658
800-571-2665

• •

TO ORDER COPIES OF

the
Adaptable Apple

Please send me _____ copies of the Adaptable Apple at $9.95 each. (Make checks payable to Hearts 'N Tummies.)
Add $3.00 S/H

Name _____

Street _____

City_____ State_____ Zip Code _____

Hearts 'N Tummies Cookbook Co.
3544 Blakslee Street
Wever, IA 52658
800-571-2665

Adaptable Apple Recipe Index

Adaptable Apple Recipe Index

Adaptable Apple Recipe Index

Adaptable Apple Recipe Index